Praise For *A View from the Roof*

"I've experienced only a few individuals in my life who possess such a captivating command of words and prose as Dr. Mackie. His disarming warmth, sincerity, and confidence allow him to challenge our most basic assumptions about ourselves and our values. Dr. Mackie succeeds in this book at doing what he does best — destroying mediocrity and apathy."

Dr. Ronald Mason
President of Jackson State University

"If not now, then when? If not Calvin Mackie, then who? We need this book. You need this book. A View from the Roof holds wonderful anecdotes and proverbs that, if understood and believed, can fundamentally alter the course of a family's history. Willie Jr., Calvin, and Anthony are a testament to their father's perseverance, diligence, skill, love, and this American life. This is a must read!"

Paul Philpott
Founder, Ben Carson Lifetime Scholars

"A View from the Roof is a candid, down-to-earth, and unpretentious conversational guide to success. There's something about Dr. Mackie's message that forces you to see things differently, to consider his arguments, and to learn from his experiences. This a great book for anyone interested in achieving personal excellence."

James E. Gibbs
Director of Human Resources
DuPont, Safety & Protection

"Over the past 20 years, I have had the pleasure of watching Dr. Mackie leverage his 'view from the roof' in his personal, spiritual, and professional life. His life story is an inspirational journey paved with the wisdom of work ethic, moral values, self worth, and persistence. This real life parable has a message for all and is applicable in business and everyday life."

Sam Johnson
Managing Partner, Business Risk Services
North Central Area of Ernst & Young

"From his father's entrepreneurial success to Calvin's relentless drive to become a doctor, *A View from the Roof* is an illuminating study in how people can always strive to become something more. Dr. Mackie deftly tackles how to achieve the American Dream in today's society through hard work, perseverance, and the cultivation of personal values. Anyone looking to achieve a fulfilling life at home and in the workplace will find this book inspiring, engrossing, and downright entertaining."

Phil Wilkins
CEO of Diverse Wealth Systems
and author of *Own Your Business, Own Your Life!*

A View from the Roof—
Lessons for Life & Business

A View from the Roof—
Lessons for Life & Business

by Calvin Mackie, Ph.D.
With stories from Willie Mackie Jr.

With a Special Forward by Anthony Mackie,
star of
Spike Lee's *She Hate Me* & *Sucker Free City*

www.AcanthusPublishing.com

Acanthus Publishing
a division of
The Ictus Group, LLC

Library of Congress Cataloging-in-Publication Data

Mackie, Calvin.
A view from the roof : lessons for life and business
/ Calvin Mackie ; with stories from Willie Mackie, Jr.,
and a special forward by Anthony Mackie.
p. cm.
Includes bibliographical references.
ISBN 0-9754810-3-7
1. Self-actualization (Psychology) 2. Life skills.
3. Success.   I. Mackie, Willie. II. Title.
BF637.S4M33 2005   158.1
QBI04-700602

Printed in the United States of America
10 9 8 7 6 5 4 3

Designed by Charisse L. Brookman

To our father, Willie Mackie, for your story is an American Story to be shared, documented, and remembered. Thank you for being a man, a father, and an inspiration. May your drive, achievements, and human imperfections continue to inspire people you have never met to accomplish what's in their hearts. By example, you continue to draw a blueprint for future generations.

To our mother, Martha, for your spirit permeates every word of every paragraph of every page of this book. Where would we be had it not been for your love, strength, and dedication to your family?

To our ancestors, who lived, fought, and died so that one day we could live!

*The author wishes to acknowledge the generous
support and encouragement of:*

My wife, Tracy, and sons, Myles and Mason, for the time necessary to think, write, and rewrite.

Anthony and Willie for sharing what is personal and private with the world for this book to be possible and complete.

My family members and friends who felt Willie Mackie's stories were worth sharing with the world, helping us to remember the importance and impact of the experiences.

My friends and mentors, Thomas J. Blocker, Dalinda Brown-Clark, Carolyn Meyers, Robert Haley, Wanda Pierson, Derrick and Sheila Scott for never accepting anything but my best and continuously pushing me to write, share, dream, and live.

Jimmie L. Davis and Aidoo Osei for your acute eyes, evaluations, and suggestions.

Mike Black, my editor at Acanthus Publishing; may my father one day get to experience the exhilaration with the New Orleans Saints you experienced this year with the Patriots and the BoSox. Thanks for your efforts.

Table of Contents

Foreword
By Anthony Mackie

One day when I was in high school, the actor Wendell Pierce came to visit our class. He was someone I greatly admired for his work on stage and in such films as *Malcolm X* and *Casualties of War,* and he was the first person from my high school to attend The Juilliard School in New York. I had a chance to meet with him privately after he spoke, and I asked him what I had to do in order to make it big like him. He said, "Study as much as possible with great teachers, never compromise, and always do the things you want to do."

Following in Wendell's footsteps, I eventually enrolled at Juilliard, where I studied with some of the best acting teachers in the world, but I knew I still had more to learn. Soon after graduation, I landed the lead role in Spike Lee's *Sucker Free City,* and I had the opportunity to learn from one of the best in the business.

Working with Spike was a life changing experience. Spike was always the first to work and the last to leave at night. I was blown away by his focused and purpose-driven energy. By the end of the second week, I was trying to beat him to work and doing extra work at the end of the day to make the character more real. On my weekends off, I would make the five-hour drive to the neighborhood in San Francisco where the film took place and chill with some of the locals in Hunter's Point. Everybody thought I was crazy. They said I should be hanging in Los Angeles on the weekends and going to the parties, not chilling in the ghetto of San Francisco. But one thing I learned in college is that there's a right and wrong time to party. After all, I was in LA to hustle, to start a career, and I wanted to take full advantage of this one-of-a-kind opportunity.

When we completed the project, Spike asked me to be the lead in his next film, *She Hate Me*. Now, it was time to party! He told me I was on the road to becoming a great actor because of the way I worked. He cracked jokes about me trying to be the next Denzel, which was the greatest compliment in the world. I wanted Spike to know at least one part of what he said was on point. I never wanted him to think of me as jaded or lazy like some other actors. Just working with him wasn't enough. I knew this was my moment, and if I hadn't worked as hard on the set, I never would have earned his respect.

That's when I realized that being good at something is never enough. There are plenty of people in the world who are just as talented or skilled as you, but very few people who can back it up with good old-fashioned hard work. People talk big in Hollywood, but it only takes a split second for real professionals—directors like Spike—to size them up and see if they walk big as well. In acting and in life, you have to match every ounce of your God-given talent with a pound of discipline and hard work if you want to stand out from the crowd.

These weren't lessons I learned on the stage or screen, or from studying with the best acting teachers at Juilliard. These were lessons drilled into me while working with my father, Willie Mackie Sr., on the rooftops of New Orleans.

My father worked at least ten hours a day. I would see him come home all dirty and tired but never beaten. He'd always talk about the value of an honest day's work — how nothing else matters as long as you get your end of the job done. I never understood what that meant until it was my turn to "Go to work with Daddy!"

Work seems so great on TV and in movies! All the women are beautiful, and everybody's telling dirty jokes and really enjoying each other's company. Well, that's not how it is in the real world, especially when you're working on one of my father's crews. I don't know if you've ever worked on a roof, but there's nothing fun about it. In the summer, New Orleans averages a temperature of a cool 95 degrees fahrenheit at mid-afternoon, with a humidity index of 98 percent! As if that wasn't bad enough, there's 600-degree tar everywhere at your feet, reflecting the sun back in your face until you're burnt to a crisp.

But I was young, eager, and a bit naïve. My father made it a point that all three of his sons had to work at least one summer on the roof with him. My older brothers, Calvin and Willie Jr., had both done it and I always wanted to be better than them, so I actually looked forward to the day I'd finally get to join my father on the roof and show them up once and for all. So on my first day of working that summer, I was up early, dressed, and ready to go. I'll never forget my dad laughing at my excitement as we jumped in the truck and headed off to work. First we made a pit stop at the corner fruit man to "put something on our stomachs" as my father would say. Then we arrived at the warehouse where all the men were waiting. As I stepped out of the truck, everyone started laughing, clapping, and pointing at me because they all thought I'd be as weak as my brothers. I took their jokes in stride—after all, they had been working with my dad since I was born—and said hello to everybody in a friendly, but defiant way.

At exactly 8 AM, my dad came out of his office and started divvying up the different assignments among the men. The sun was just starting to creep its way high into the sky, so it wasn't really that hot yet, and I thought the day's work would be a breeze. Before I knew it, I was jumping in the back of the truck and heading off to work with a group of hard men, some 30 years my senior. As soon as we arrived at the job site, a foreman with the same name and nickname as me started barking out orders to the crew. Amazingly, everyone seemed to know their positions right off the bat, and in a matter of seconds, they were working together like a well-oiled machine. I stood and watched as four men ripped the roof off the house and two other men started unloading materials. Then Anthony, the foreman, handed me a hammer and told me to follow him. My orders for the day were to hold the ladder for the men going up and down, and use the back of the hammer to cut the seal off the supplies. I was pissed because Anthony refused to allow me on the roof. "I'm not about to let you fall off and kill yourself on my watch," he said.

As the day went on, the men worked really hard and I faded in and out of sleep by the ladder in the shade. Around noon, my father drove by making his daily rounds and was less than happy to see his youngest son asleep on the job. He walked over to me, pulled me off the ground by my collar, and had me up on the roof in a matter of minutes. By now, it was the hottest part of the day. My dad, now "Boss," gave me the work of three men to do for the rest of the afternoon. By the end of the day, my back, feet, and head were swollen and in immeasurable pain. I had finally experienced first hand what my father meant all those years about "a hard day's work." Believe me, it was a tough lesson to learn.

The end of the summer came sooner than expected, and by my last day of work, I was dirty, tired, and hating life. Everyone said goodbye and congratulated me for being much better than my brothers. Before we left for home that night, my dad sat me down in the back of his truck and began to give me a long speech as we shared our first beer together. He talked about how lucky I was to have my two older brothers and how they worked on the roof and then went on to great achievements through education. He told me that he put us all on the roof not to find our future careers, but to show us how hard life would be without an education. Then he said he never wanted to see me on a roof again unless it was by choice, and not because I couldn't do anything else. "I worked hard just to give you boys the chance to do whatever it was you wanted, and you shouldn't take that lightly," he gently noted. We sat for a minute, and then he turned to me and said, "As long as you're doing right, I'll do whatever I can for you." We shook hands, he told me he loved me, and that was the end of my summer on the roof. I worked the following summer with my dad, and then never stepped foot on a roof again!

Those two summers on the roof let me know how fortunate I was to have my father in my life. He was there to keep me honest about right and wrong and to show me how to treat people on all different levels. But the most important lesson I learned from him was how to be a man, something I couldn't get from my mother, uncles, brothers, or deacons in church. Being a man, my father taught me, had nothing to do with comparing yourself to another; being a man meant being content and focused on your own path, and continuing to grow and learn through hard work.

There's no value I can place on the humbleness I learned by watching my dad work. I saw the way he interacted with people, white and black, and the different ways he'd talk to men and women would always make me laugh. "Look 'em in the eye and they have to listen to you," he always said. "Talk slow so they know you know what you're talking about." Sure enough, he would start every conversation with a handshake followed by a Mr. or Mrs. so and so. He would ask people questions I knew he had the answers to just to make them feel comfortable. After negotiating or dealing with a customer, he'd often ask me how I would handle things differently, with all of my education. He'd listen intently to my answers and say, "If I had your education, I'd be the richest man in the world!" Before I left for college I realized that one sentence contained the most truth he had ever spoken.

Growing up, I would always hear stories of my Grandpa, a lifelong sharecropper, and how he would tell my dad he worked hard so that hopefully, one day, his children would study to be doctors and lawyers. Today my daddy often says he must have done something right because his father's dreams are coming true with his six children.

I never thought the lessons from those two summers on the roof would translate to my present profession, just as I'm sure my Grandpa never thought any of his grandkids would ever go away to boarding school and spend four years in college studying acting. I definitely know my daddy never expected he would one day be able go to the movies and see his son. But the way I see it, the three years of training in New Orleans, the one year of training in boarding school in North Carolina, and the four years of training in New York mean nothing without the two summers of training I got with my dad on the roof. I may have learned the craft of acting from some of the finest teachers in the world at these other places, but I learned the craft of living on the roof, because that's where my father taught me how to work. "Never give anybody a window to compare you," he would say. "Never give them the option to say no."

There's no way my brother Calvin can explain in these pages the full effect our father had on our lives, with his hard love and few words. What he has attempted to do is give you a window into the life and amazing lessons taught to us by our dad. It was always a learning experience to be around him. He would be the first to ask a question and the first to give an answer. He never felt sorry for himself because of his lack of formal education. What he did was give that self-confidence to his children in the form of opportunity.

There was nothing we were told we couldn't do. There was nothing we tried to do without receiving his fullest support. Because of all of this, he has been able to raise three sons, each of whom have earned degrees from some of the most selective universities in the country, and three of the strongest women in the world as daughters. I hope you are able to rejoice in the stories and lessons of my daddy, Willie Mackie, as we have all our lives. His wisdom will lead you to success, if not a leading role. Enjoy!

Anthony Dwane "Doodie" Mackie
Los Angeles
November 29, 2004

Introduction

I recently visited the White House to receive an award from President George W. Bush and the National Science Foundation for my work mentoring young adults in science, math, and engineering. Before leaving for the trip, I called my father to tell him I was headed to the White House. "That's where you're supposed to be!" he replied with a chuckle.

That kind of response is typical for my father, Willie Mackie Sr., who holds everyone around him, especially his children, to the highest expectations. Without my father's unwavering faith and optimism in my abilities, and his commitment to teaching me how to be the most successful person I could be in life and in business, I never would have made it to the White House, except maybe on a public tour. It may seem cliché to say this, but I owe the award, and much of my success, to him. He was my greatest teacher and continues to be to this day.

I wrote this book as a way to honor and celebrate the core philosophies, lessons, and values my father instilled in my brothers and me for success, and to impart some of his priceless wisdom at a time when America could use it most.

As I write this now, low expectations are crippling the children and working professionals of this country. I look around and see so many people who have lost the intelligence, drive, tenacity, and sheer intestinal fortitude to overcome even the most minimal obstacles before them. We have over 100,000 soldiers in Iraq now fighting to give Iraqi children the same opportunities that our children have here, though our children choose to squander them. America is presently facing an unparalleled crisis in education. We no longer understand the purpose of education, nor do we value our need as human beings for self-determination and actualization. We are fast becoming a nation of what I call the "walking, breathing, living dead."

I wrote this book as a wake-up call for change — first in our own attitudes and perceptions of the world, and secondly in the way we approach and teach the next generation. We can no longer afford to watch education fall by the wayside. As my father would say, "It's time to stop goofing off and get back to work."

As a nation we have taken our freedoms, our liberties, and our abundance of educational and economic opportunities for granted. In doing so, we have forgotten and paid ill tribute to the past. There was a time in America not long ago when the opportunities we enjoy today were considered luxuries of the upper classes, and closed off entirely to other people because of the color of their skin.

During and immediately after World War I, many southern blacks migrated to the northern United States seeking to escape the impoverishment of the rural south. With foreign immigration suspended due to the war, northern companies needed and heavily recruited unskilled southern labor. Most southern blacks were sharecroppers who planted and picked cotton, one of the most labor-intensive field crops ever known to man. Southern blacks continued migrating north as economic and living conditions worsened, but many decided to remain close to home and live under the vicious segregation laws of Jim Crow, which were backed up by a reign of terror that offered blacks substandard education and primitive living conditions.

Such harsh conditions continued through World War II and into the late '40s. Many black servicemen who had fought for the freedom of other nations overseas returned home and intensified their challenge to the virtual servitude and segregation statutes imposed by the Jim Crow laws. By any standards in the history of the world and definitely the history of the United States, the basic tenets of the Jim Crow South were inhumane. To this day they remain a permanent stain on the fabric of America.

People such as my father, who were born and lived before the Civil Rights era, will never forget the pain, suffering, and second-class treatment they received in a free country. Men were unable to live as men, forced to attend sub-standard schools with secondhand books, denied the right to vote, subject to taxation without representation, and unfairly accused or wrongly punished for crimes they didn't commit. It was even considered a norm in society to address a black man as "boy." How do you gain a healthy self-esteem and believe that the promise of America is also for you, when you're not allowed the basic dignity of developing as a human being? How does a flower grow through the concrete created to stunt its growth and destroy its seeds?

W.E.B. DuBois answered these rhetorical questions when he said, "There is in this world no such force as the force of a man determined to rise. The human soul cannot be permanently chained."

My father is one of the many individuals from his generation who has proven DuBois right. These individuals represent everything that is good, great, and becoming of a life well lived. They have defied the odds and achieved feats no one would have predicted. Their names may never appear in lights and their stories may never be told, but their influence will touch and teach generations yet unborn. Through their trials and tribulations, we learn to live every day, every hour, and every minute with zeal and zest.

This book is a tribute to anyone who started life with low expectations, and through strength, perseverance, and hard work, raised him — or herself — to the top. My father is a living embodiment of their struggles, a shining example of what we call The Promise of America. He did not allow society or his social, economic, political, or racial conditions to rob him of his inalienable right to life, liberty, and happiness. His soul could not be held down by the cowardly and self-serving fabricated barriers other human beings constructed in his way. He likewise refused to allow his children to believe that there were limits to their potentials. Every time I travel, continentally or internationally, I call and wait for him to ask, "Where are you?" When I give him a name, his standard response warms my heart: "That's where you belong ... go around the world, boy." My father's expectations for the people around him always supersede what they themselves believe they can achieve.

Although he was never formally educated, my father is speaking to the world through his children. In 1988, my brother Willie Mackie Jr. graduated from the University of Louisiana with a Bachelor of Science degree in Business Administration. He made a name for himself in the restaurant circles of New Orleans, serving in various managerial positions. Currently, Willie Mackie is pursuing the same success in the automotive sales industry. Anthony Mackie, the youngest son and brother, attended The Julliard School of Performing Arts in New York City, graduating in 2001. Since then, he has appeared on Broadway three times opposite stars such as Whoopi Goldberg, Charles Dutton, and Alfre Woodard. At the age of 25, Anthony has already worked with Spike Lee, Clint Eastwood, Denzel Washington, and Samuel L. Jackson. Today, I am a professional speaker and college professor with four degrees, including a doctoral degree in mechanical engineering. I teach at Tulane University, one of the top private universities in the country, and have a successful educational consulting firm, Channel Zer0, that allows me to impact young adults across the world.

I know we did not arrive at these positions by chance or accident. Our success has come from design, through the masterful direction and examples of Willie Mackie Sr. Together, we are all speaking to the world in our own way, and you will be able to hear our father's words through our own as you read on through the book.

A View from the Roof is a road map and virtual Blackberry™ of lessons that will inspire and direct your lives to personal greatness. Society demands that we be successful, but it doesn't offer sufficient and ample direction. A View from the Roof teaches us how to become successful. The stories are real. The lessons are from the soul. They are transferable and replicable. Working on the roof with my father, I learned to see things other people could not see. From high-rise buildings, I saw that no matter where you lived in the city, regardless of your education or socio-economic position, there were always roads that led out of the darkness of despair and into the light of a promising future. The view from the roof always gave me hope, and the lessons I learned up there were the fuel for the soul that allowed me to make my sojourn in life.

I hope this book allows you to stand on the roof and absorb the magnanimous view. May the stories and lessons generate hope and fuel for your soul as well.

Dr. Calvin Mackie
New Orleans
November 26, 2004

Create Something Out of Nothing:
Master Your Craft

DDCIELLD

My father was very excited when I went to college, although he wasn't happy that I chose to go 500 miles away in Atlanta. He would've preferred that I remain in New Orleans where I could help him with his roofing business. He wanted me to learn it from the inside out and eventually run it one day. But he was still glad to see me get the education he never got in life.

> *"I know of no more encouraging fact than*
> *the unquestionable ability of man to elevate*
> *himself by conscious endeavor."*
>
> – Henry David Thoreau

My road trips back home were the greatest. My college friends loved to travel to New Orleans and sample the exotic food and, of course, meet the beautiful women. We had the itinerary completely laid out from the time we rolled into the city on Friday to the time we left the following Sunday, hung-over and exhausted.

Once in New Orleans, we'd make a beeline directly to my house where my mother would be anxiously awaiting us. Pulling into the driveway, we'd smell the deep fried chicken and that classic New Orleans staple, red beans and rice. We'd greet my mom with hugs and kisses, and start devouring the food like there was no tomorrow. She'd watch us, making sure everyone was okay and everything was spectacular. My friend and roommate, Jimmie, didn't drink, but the rest of us did — and whatever we drank those nights always came to us in super-sized proportions.

We'd joke around and play with other family members while we ate, and people would pass in and out of the house constantly. It seemed like the entire extended family, and sometimes the whole neighborhood, would make it through the door on those nights when they knew I was coming home.

One of the best treats for my friends was the opportunity to interact with my father. The entire mood of the house changed when he entered the door. It was clear that this was his castle and he was the king. He'd come into the kitchen and everyone, especially my mom, would hustle to make sure his place at the table was clear and a hot plate of food was on its way.

Seated at his throne at the head of the dinner table, my father would try to stump the "high-minded" college kids while we ate. Using a great big drumstick as a pointer, he'd often challenge us from as many different perspectives as he could, testing to see how his eighth-grade education measured up next to our fancy college-trained minds.

One memorable evening we were sitting in the spacious den around the oak coffee table. The Budweiser was flowing and my dad was in rare form. He started telling us the story about his dad and how he couldn't attend school because he was a sharecropper. Being the son of a sharecropper, my father likewise spent most of his day, from sun up to sun down, working his butt off in the cotton fields so his family would have enough money to put food on the table. He didn't have time for the fun and education we were enjoying away at school.

My father told us that my grandfather would pick potatoes, cotton, and other staples and bring them to the markets in the morning for the merchants to buy. At the market, he had to address everyone as "Mister," despite the fact that he was much older than the white male merchants doing the purchasing.

After selling his produce, my grandfather would stand there counting his money, beaming with pride. Then he'd always turn to my father and say, "You see, son, I am a DD-C-I-E-LL-D (double D, C-I-E, LL-D)."

My father teased us and told us that with all of our degrees and college education we'd never be able figure out the meaning of that word. Of course we accepted his statement as a challenge. Putting our collective college brains together, we studied the word, wrote it down, attempted to find its Latin roots, and tried to say it phonetically. We did everything our English teachers taught us to do when confronted with obscure vocabulary, but we just couldn't make any sense of that word, let alone pronounce it. It wasn't like any word we'd ever seen before.

My father laid back into the sofa and sipped his Bud. With great satisfaction he said, "You see, I am a DDCIELLD like my father. Someday, if you're lucky, maybe you boys will be one too." We had no idea what my father meant, but each time my friends visited, he'd tell the same exact story over and over again, and we'd try harder and harder every time to define that mystery word, DDCIELLD.

Years went by and we still had no idea what he was attempting to say, or spell for that matter. This continued as my college friends, and eventually my graduate school friends, came home with me to experience the sights and smells of New Orleans.

One night my father recounted the story as usual and after everyone finished laughing, I finally said, "Dad, you know you always tell us that story. We've spent years and years trying to figure out what that word means, and collectively we have come up with nothing. So, what are you saying?"

My father paused for a moment. Then he finally revealed his secret. "You see," he said, "our grandfather and his father lived during a time in America when black men were not allowed to attend school, or get the degrees and titles their white counterparts had. But your grand-father knew that he had mastered his trade and his craft. He decided his mastery should be called something special, so he called it 'DDCI-ELLD.' 'DDCIELLD' means you have mastered your craft — that you are 'The Highest.'"

My father then told us that having been a roofer for over 40 years, he was officially a DDCIELLD — "The Highest" in his craft — and that all he can do now is pass his knowledge on to others as his father had done.

On our trip back to Atlanta, my friends and I discussed the entire issue, and had a good laugh at my father. And then suddenly it hit me.

There we were, three young men driving to Atlanta, returning to our Ph.D. studies in our respective areas. Growing up, my father and his father didn't have such an opportunity, so out of nothing they created something — a name, a moniker — that signified their experience and accomplishment. The law didn't allow them to have the titles that are ordained and associated with higher institutions in America, just as my wise and seasoned grandfather could never be honored even with the simple title of "Mister" from white men far less than half his age; and yet he didn't let this insult deter him from achieving mastery of his craft.

At first I thought that someone might think it was stupid of my grandfather to invent his own degree, but the more I thought about it, the more proud I felt. It started to make sense. After all, I pondered, what did the man possess who issued the first Ph.D. degree? It certainly wasn't a Ph.D. Someone created this degree out of these three letters to be conferred to individuals who have attained a certain level of mastery in a specific field. The DDCIELLD degree my grandfather invented wasn't any different.

Many years have passed since my father first told my friends and I that story. I have since attained my Ph.D. degree, but I still haven't received my DDCIELLD. Those letters mean absolute mastery, and I've only just begun to master my craft. Mastery takes time. It isn't just a matter of graduating from college or getting your degree. You have to spend many years honing your skills to perfection. As a matter of fact, my father reminds me every day that I am not there yet, and that I have a long way to go before I can call myself a master.

Those Who Master a Craft
Define Success on Their Own Terms

Creating something out of nothing seems to be my family calling, our legacy.

My father started his roofing company with a ladder on top of a truck and built it into a thriving urban business with over 100 employees. His goal was to become a DDCIELLD — a master of his craft like his father. The experiences of my father and grandfather validate Booker T. Washington's belief that a man or a woman who can supply something this world needs will find success regardless of their race, sex, or gender.

Master a craft and then offer it to the world. If you're the only one offering it then the world has no choice but to come to you, but if you have competitors, you must separate your services from theirs, and the best way to accomplish this is through the quality of your work. The integrity and quality of your craftsmanship will be your cutting edge advantage in an increasingly competitive world. At the end of the day, a customer will call you because they know what they're going to receive each and every time: quality. Someone else may offer the service or product for less money, but if it doesn't measure up for quality, it will show every time.

My father often repeats the saying, "Call me now or call me later, pay someone else now or pay me later, the choice is yours." He drove this home to his children and continues to drive it into us on a daily basis. Be your best, do your best, get up in the morning, and go do something somewhere. Eventually society will recognize you as a master of your craft. Then you'll be in a position to pick and choose the work you want to do, and be called upon to teach and direct others who desire to participate in your industry. You'll become a master teacher, a leading authority, and a keeper of the craft.

You may be asking yourself, "How can I master a craft or create something from nothing?" That's a very valid question.

Mastery of anything isn't easy. It starts with a decision: a decision to make tomorrow different from today. Life places no greater burden on a man or woman than that of making a decision. Most people refuse to make decisions because they don't want to take responsibility for the decision's repercussions once it has been made. Instead of grabbing control of present circumstances and creating a course for the future, they allow fate to just happen. This is a sad use of the bountiful opportunities we are lucky to have in America, where we have the freedom to get up every morning and chart a course for ourselves and for future generations. Our destiny is in our hands. We have the inalienable right to pursue our happiness, which is given to us by God and protected by the sacred document called *The Constitution of the United States of America*.

In America, we're supposed to create something out of nothing. The doors to mastery are wide open, and we must walk through these doors if we expect to survive in the 21st century. In America and in the world, competency alone is no longer something to aspire to. Good enough is no longer good enough. To compete in the world now you have to be exceptional. Mastery comes from going beyond good enough and knowing more than enough all the time.

Business coach Thomas Leonard says that mastery is really the manifestation of three different areas: knowledge, skill, and awareness.* Mas-

---

* Thomas Leonard and Byron Larsen. *The Portable Coach*. New York: Scribner, 1998.

tery occurs when these traits exist at the same time. We need to have knowledge, but knowledge alone isn't mastery. Being able to regurgitate facts and figures in your craft is a nice start, but you need more. In America, we all need skills so that we can barter with each other and produce income to survive, but that doesn't make you a master of the craft. You're just someone who can perform the task.

The ultimate trait of mastery is awareness. Too many people today are walking around unaware of their surroundings, unaware of the past, unaware of the present, and blind to the future. They have the skills and knowledge to succeed, but don't know how to use these gifts to transform humankind and make this world a better place for the future. To achieve mastery, you have to be aware of your environment: this way you can better access the needs and desires of your environment.

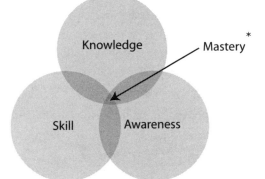

Couple an awareness of your environment with knowledge and skills, and you'll be able to create something, or master a service, the universe has never witnessed before.

---

* Illustration based upon Thomas Leonard's "28 Principles of Attraction." Ibid.

Six Steps Towards Mastering Your Craft

Here are some ways to achieve mastery of your craft:

1 Find something you like to do or would do for free

I often visit hobby shops, craft stores, flower stores, and other service-oriented businesses and ask the owners how they arrived at this place. The typical response I hear is, "I've always loved to do this on the side, so I finally decided to quit my job and make this my career."

Somehow we've been trained to believe that a career should be something that results from some formal study or degree, but it's a fact that many formally educated people are unhappy because they've been domesticated and ripped away from their true happiness and place of competitive advantage. Think about it: The things we do happily we do better and longer. Many people spend a lifetime working at jobs they hate and spend their weekends doing things they really enjoy.

What action, task, or hobby brings a smile to your face? Maybe this is what you should be doing. Have you ever considered turning your hobby or habit into a profitable entity?

I have a friend who's a trained scientist, but it's obvious to everyone that her real talent lies in the production of creative gifts and cards. Every time she creates a new setting, or plans the design for a party, people are truly in awe. She loves doing these types of activities, and because she's so good, she's presented with more opportunities to do them. She doesn't see the potential, however, to direct her talents toward creating a sustaining profitable career where she's both happy and free. She does better work than many of her competitors, but she doesn't charge competitive rates for her work. Her creative skills are what make her happy and she's literally exercising them for free. What can I say? She's a caring, kind person, but she's letting the goodness of her heart cloud the business opportunity and career prospect right before her eyes.

2 Do something that comes easily or naturally to you

Making creative gifts and designing and planning parties are talents that come easy to my friend. I, on other hand, have no artistic skill whatsoever. I'm more than willing to pay someone with such God-given gifts to perform these tasks for me. Party and event planning is a multibillion dollar industry for the very reason that few people have the skills my friend possesses.

Interestingly, I have another friend who has a national event planning business. The creative and organizational skills required for this career come very naturally to him. Unlike my other friend in the same field, he's willing to turn his passion into profit. Here are two friends who view their God-given talents very differently. One friend sees opportunity, happiness, and financial freedom; the other only sees a hobby.

Take some time right now to ask yourself this question: "What comes easy or naturally to me?" The promise of America is the freedom to pursue opportunity, and the easy task may be the opportunity you should be pursuing on a daily basis.

Many athletes are freaks of nature; the abilities to run fast, jump high, or throw hard come natural to them. They're equipped with intrinsic physical advantages over other individuals.

We're enamored of sports figures because many of us have dreamt of being the next star. We know how difficult it is to mirror the feats of athletes. But what Tiger is to golf, Jordan is to basketball, Gretsky is to hockey, and A-Rod is to baseball, you may be to engineering, mathematics, marketing, speaking, teaching, etc. We're all secretly "freaks of nature" at something. Jordan was born with some talents the rest of us don't have, but I know I can run loops around Jordan, Tiger, and A-Rod when it comes to math and physics. These are talents that come naturally and easily to me, so I have sought to master them at every opportunity.

What are your gifts? What are your strengths? What comes naturally or easily to you? Find them, master them, and make them your career.

3 Understand that sleep is overrated

Sleep is overrated. My father always says, "The only thing that comes to a sleeper is a dream." A Senegalese proverb says, "The opportunity that God brings does not wake he who is asleep."

Your goal must be to wake up and start the action necessary to make your dreams come true. Often, this is accomplished while others are sleeping. Are you willing to work harder and longer than anyone else? If so, you're prepared to meet with the kinds of success others will never meet with in their lifetime.

Of course all of us need rest. I'm simply saying that you must fill every waking minute with effort spent toward mastering your newfound skill, the one that brings you joy and comes easily to you. Don't forget that other individuals are also working hard. In school, I knew people who possessed photographic memories as well as other natural talents I lacked. But guess what? Every day I was committed to outworking everyone and that attitude empowered me to outshine the rest in everything I did.

To become a true master you have to stop thinking of work in terms of 9 to 5. This is one of the most important lessons I learned from my father.

I remember working on a roofing job with my dad as a kid. The day had been brutally hot, and we'd been sweating on that roof for eight hours without a break. As the evening approached and the darkness started to set in, I began whining that I wanted to go home. I'll never forget the stern look on my father's face. He told me in a very terse voice that this was his business and he had to complete the job. It didn't matter if it took until midnight; he had a job to do.

Having an expansive work ethic is essential if you want to become a noted master in your industry. Discipline, determination, and proficiency come from sticking with the task to the end. When you can start a task and see it through to completion, you're on your way to mastering your craft. Remember the adage: "The race is not won by the swiftest or the strongest but by he or she who endures to the end."

Your eternity is in your time. Use every minute wisely because it's free and you can't get it back when it's gone.

4 Read, listen, and study the present masters in your area or related area

Look around at other people performing at the top of their games. Study their habits and work ethic. Mirror their attitudes and behaviors. Success is learned just like anything else. You can learn and apply the habits of other people and effect change in your own life.

I studied a lot in school, often reading and re-reading the same information repeatedly. It was clear I knew the material, but I always wanted to be certain. There was one kid in this upper level math course that would outscore everyone on every test. I had nicknamed him "The Crusher" because he literally "crushed" every test, scoring near perfect.

One day I saw him at the library seated at the end of my table. I slid over to him and whispered, "Whassuupp, Crusher?" He just looked at me, smiled, and responded, "Nothin'."

I was curious because we had one of the biggest math tests of the year coming up. "What are you doing? Studying?" I asked. "Nope, I'm just reading the comics," he said.

Now I was even more curious because I was beginning to wonder if Crusher had started to slip. So I asked him, "Crusher, tell me the truth, how much do you study to get the grades you're getting?"

I'll never forget his response. He said, "I don't study that much. I think a lot!" Damn, his words messed me up, and I had to sit there and think for a second, re-evaluating everything. I asked myself, "Do I study a lot, or do I think a lot?"

Well, I began spending more time thinking about the things I read and studied instead of just reading and re-reading the facts. I spent more time synthesizing different aspects of the theories instead of memorizing them as separate parts. Sure enough, my grades began to climb higher and higher, my understanding became clearer, and my confidence in this highly technical subject began to grow.

13

The Crusher had revealed a deep secret to me: "The man who out-thinks you, rules you!" I needed more than knowledge and facts; I needed to be able to analyze and integrate this knowledge into theory and application. From that point forward I began studying individuals to determine what makes them special. Now when I see someone successful, I immediately ask, "What are his or her secrets to success and achievement?" Then I ask, "How can I incorporate these skills into my life to help me increase my skills and better master my craft?" Finally, I wake up and get to work becoming a better individual and professional.

"Do not seek to follow in the footsteps of the men of old; seek what they sought."

– Matsuo Basho,
haiku poet, 4th century B.C.

But listen. Don't attempt to become someone else or redo what he or she has already accomplished. Seek the level of truth and excellence they sought in their work in your own life and endeavors. You can only be second best at being someone else. Genius is within us all; we should all strive to give birth to it.

5 Accept failure and criticism as an opportunity to learn, grow, and get better

The only certainty in life, excluding death and taxes, is that you will fail at something. Most successes, in fact, only occur after we fall flat on our faces.

14

When you seek the advice of masters, you must open yourself to receive brutal but honest criticism. I'm speaking of critical advice given in the spirit of helping you improve. There will always be those naysayers (some of them very close to you) who just don't believe in you. They'll say negative things to destroy your efforts and motivation. You have to do your best to exclude those individuals and weigh what they say with a grain of salt. Seek those individuals you respect and receive their evaluations and feedback with the spirit in which it's given. Many individuals nowadays have developed the habit of taking everything personally. When you're trying to master your craft, criticism is never personal. When someone rejects your idea, keep in mind that he or she is rejecting the idea, and not you, the person.

Grow a thick shield of skin because when you put yourself out there, you may not be happy with the comments you receive. Keep your head up and go back to the drawing board.

The wildly successful reality show "American Idol" is the best example I can present of critical advice in action. Most of the contestants are living pipe dreams. They don't know how much talent it really takes to become a star in the music industry. Many simply lack talent altogether, or they have decent voices, but are missing the professional voice training to be exceptional. Nevertheless, their families, friends, and communities have told them that they're talented and should pursue a career in singing. Every week when we turn on the television and watch the hearts of these brave individuals being ripped out by the brutal truth of professional industry masters and judges, it's only natural to cringe a bit and begin questioning our professed qualifications in our own field.

Aim high, but be honest. Consider whether you're personally blessed or gifted to pursue the craft you want to master. Being truthful with yourself can help you avoid the pain of criticism and abject failure. Let's face it: You and I will probably never be successful singers, rappers, athletes, or dancers. So let's throw away those pipe dreams, discover our true callings, and begin mastering them to perfection. We can't afford to waste time.

I know deep down criticism hurts. You've committed your waking minutes, hours, days, and weeks to a creation or task, only to have it slammed by the experts. The criticism, however, will provide a roadmap for where you should expend more energy and effort. It may direct you to seek additional training and preparation in one particular area of your craft and help you focus. No one is good at everything.

6 Raise at least one standard or expectation in your field or industry

My father has a habit of consistently giving people more than they expect or pay for. In Louisiana, we call it lagniappe, a little something extra. Always go the extra mile when performing your craft. People appreciate it, but more importantly, they'll tell someone else.

You know you've mastered a craft when you raise the bar of what's expected for others in the industry. Tiger Woods has accomplished feats in golf others thought were impossible. His mastery has subtly forced other golfers to raise their game to a level they didn't know existed. Mediocre golfers now have to push themselves to become exceptional if they want to take on Tiger.

You don't have to dominate like Tiger to raise or create another standard in your field, but you can personalize the standard, so that every time you perform your craft your customer responds with "I've never seen it done like that before" or "I've never gotten so much for so little." The industry will begin to notice the new and exciting things you're bringing to the field, and that's when people will begin to invite you to speak, to perform, to give seminars, and to teach the rest of the world how you do it. Raise your standard of excellence higher than any standard anyone else can have for you, and soon you'll change the expectations for an entire industry.

Tom Joyner was a regular morning radio talk show host who was doing great in Chicago when he was offered a prime evening ride home spot in Dallas. Instead of making a choice between the two, he decided to do them both, flying between both cities and broadcasting twice a day. He raised the standard for radio talk show hosts and earned the moniker "The Fly Jock." The rest is history. He's now heard across the country as a morning and evening drive time syndicated radio host.

Raise the standard of excellence by working hard, staying focused, and going beyond the expected in everything you do. You'll not only become a master at your craft, you'll transform the world.

WILLIE'S VIEW

When I was very young, my sister and I started our own business selling icebergs, or frozen Kool-Aid pops, out of our home.

We started our business because we weren't satisfied with the product we were getting from people in the neighborhood. Other kids sold the same frozen treat, but their icebergs weren't as tasty or as large as we wanted them to be, so we started producing them ourselves.

My father gave us a stern warning about our venture. He said, "Once you start doin' this you'll have to see it through. There won't be any time that you can't want to do this." Then he asked us why we wanted to do this anyway. We told him we wanted to make our own money for the summer, but the truth of the matter was that we didn't care about the money we were getting, we just wanted to eat free icebergs.

When we started our business we offered larger cups and more flavors than our competitors. This was my dad's idea. He said if we were going to be more successful than the other guys we'd have to offer something different. "Just look," he said, "everyone's selling only two colors of icebergs. You've gotta offer more." So we did. My sister and I felt that we needed something else, so we dropped a gumball in the bottom of each cup before we froze it. This way you'd have a special treat when you flipped the contents of the frozen cup inside out.

Our concept was so successful, people from every block came to our home to buy our cups. Soon word got out and we were in business.

By giving us these tips, my dad was trying, in his own way, to teach us the concept of competition in business, the idea of what it takes to be ahead of the game. This lesson is still with me today.

One day during our iceberg summer, my sister and I wanted to leave home to visit and spend the weekend with our cousins. This was something we always did. On this particular weekend, however, my dad stepped in and said no to our sleepover. He told us that since we'd started the iceberg business, we'd have to continue it no matter what. This came as a blow to all of our weekend plans because at least one of us had to be home to tend to the kids who would come for the icebergs. My father wouldn't let us quit the job we started.

It wasn't until later on in life I realized just how important that ruined weekend was to me. It gave me an inner sense of responsibility that stuck with me always.

Nothing is Greater Than
Education, Training, & Experience

The Sharecropper's Education

Deep in my heart I believe my father's drive to accomplish something tangible in this world grew out of his lack of opportunity to attain a formal education. As kids he often told us that all he ever wanted was to be able to sit down and read a book from cover to cover, something I don't think he's accomplished even to this day.

My father was one of 14 children growing up in a post-slavery Jim Crow agricultural economy where cotton was still king, and where cheap labor was still needed to pick it. Even today you can drive down Louisiana State Highway 66 and see the big plantations and farms where my father's family worked. Looking at the land with sprawling tractors and fancy watering systems dancing between the rows of corn, peanuts, greens, beans, potatoes, and other vegetation, you have to wonder how these farms operated before the era of technology. Considering that the natural heat coupled with the Louisiana humidity is almost unbearable to the common man, you also have to wonder how many people perished in those fields for pennies a day in an attempt to make a living. Most of the rich land is still owned by the same slave-holding Jim Crow era families of the past. Their children never had to work those fields from sun up to sun down the way many of my ancestors did.

Growing up, my family would often drive on the narrow two-lane back roads through the woods passing the plantations like Live Oak, where my mother worked, and Greenwood, where my father worked. As we drove, my father would describe for us the pain of having to walk miles to school with the same clothes on every day while watching the school bus of white children pass him by. He told us how he and his siblings had to walk past the new brick school for whites to attend the old dilapidated schoolhouse which employed outdated secondhand textbooks left over from the white school. He'd explain how he was unable to answer questions when called upon by his teacher because his absences were more numerous than the days he attended, and that he often felt ashamed for having to miss class to work in the field. Eventually, the pain, disgust, indignation, and frustration grew too great to bear and he succumbed to the nature of his environment.

Like many African-Americans of his time growing up in the rural south, my father watched with hawkish eyes and waited with glee for the day when he'd be able to escape the black hole in which he found himself buried. Somewhere between sixth and eighth grade, he realized that school and formal education wouldn't be his ticket out of those fields. With very little formal education, he knew he had to make a way with his hands, so he entered the roofing profession and never looked back.

In spite of his own upbringing, my father in his wisdom always understood that though he had succeeded with his hands at a trade, his children deserved a formal education. He pushed us all, therefore, to learn everything we could. The way he saw it, his job was to provide for the family and our job was to go to school. If he had mastered his craft by working day and night, weekends and holidays, he expected the same kind of commitment out of us.

Bringing my report card home as a kid was always a challenge because my father was such an intense critic. My mother would always look at my report card and ask me, "Did you do your best?" I'd reply, "Yes" and she'd simply say, "Well done!" My father, on the other hand, never seemed satisfied. I'd have all A's and one B on my report card and he'd turn around and ask, "What happened here?" I'd ask him what he meant by that, and he'd point out that I had one B, which meant there was room for improvement. "Damn!" I'd think to myself as I walked away, "Is anything good enough for this man?"

My father often joked that the only time he received A's and B's in school was A for Absent and B for Boy! He knew he wasn't a great scholar, but he expected me to do better than he did in class, or not go at all. Even to this day, he'll still say to me, "Boy, if I could read and write like you, I'd be a billionaire."

. . . .

"When planning for a year, plant corn. When planning for a decade, plant trees. When planning for life, train and educate people."

– Chinese proverb:
Guanzi (c. 645 B.C.)

. . . .

Eventually, because of his hard work, my father has been able to send all six of his children to college, with four completing a degree. I received the highest degree this country has to offer — a Doctorate of Philosophy. But he often warns us even to this day that formal education isn't enough. The experience we receive in the real world, he says, must be the ultimate teacher. There is no substitute for experience, or doing the job firsthand. Education will help you understand many principles and the way things ought to work, but experience — the application of your education — will truly test your mettle, he says.

I know what an on-the-job education was like for my father. Every summer I worked on the roof with my dad's company. We toiled through grueling eight to ten hours days, where the 90-100 degree temperatures and 80-90 percent humidity created a heat index wavering between 100 to 110 degrees. This has been my father's life for 40 years, a life that has allowed him to make a very decent living and raise a family of eight. He never wanted this type of hard labor for his children, but he understood the lessons that such a life had taught him, and has attempted to transfer those lessons to us in the form of work ethic and discipline.

In the end, my father only wanted us to do our best and he made it very clear that this meant building our lives, not his. As a parent, he wanted to make sure his children had the opportunity to create a way for themselves in this world beyond hard labor jobs, such as roofing or picking cotton. However, he often made it known that he'd still be very proud of us if we preferred to do a manual labor, blue-collar job. He wasn't ashamed of what he did and encouraged us to pursue our dreams any way we wanted, as long as we pursued them with passion.

Get Education, Training, and Exposure First and Everything Else Will Fall Into Place

Granted, my father realizes that life is the ultimate educator, but he has also felt limited at times by his lack of formal education. He'll readily admit that many of his struggles in life and business were due to the fact that he didn't receive a college degree. But he doesn't narrowly define education as schooling either. He understands that formal education needs the tempering of experience. To him, education is a complete package, encompassing utility, morality, intelligence, and culture.

The purpose of education

Plato says that it's the purpose given to education that will define mostly everything that follows. My father defines education in a similarly broad sense.

Today, many people believe that the purpose of education is to get a good job and to make good money. This myopic view has created a trend that is leading America down a slippery slope of materialism, greed, and immorality. We live in a country where there are 100 million ways to make money and earn a living, all without a formal education. If we accept this materialistic educational paradigm as gospel then anyone earning money is justified in his or her moneymaking endeavor, regardless of the evil or pain it causes. Thus every pimp, drug pusher, thief, unethical public official, and all others earning money by exploiting our children, destroying our communities, and selling unmitigated consumerism and greed, should be allowed to exist unencumbered by the law or society.

The purpose of education isn't to make money, but to supply you with the tools and mechanisms to be free: free to create, free to produce, and free to do the things God has ordained and created you to do. As W.E.B. DuBois stated, the purpose of education is not to make men and women into doctors, lawyers, and engineers, but to make doctors, lawyers, and engineers into men and women. After all, it's our ability to think and make decisions that separates us from the animal kingdom. It's through education that we develop and expand upon these capacities. Education, therefore, not only gives us skills, it helps to increase our sense of "somebodiness."

Martin Luther King Jr. wrestled with the meaning of education long before America knew his name. In 1948, as a student at Morehouse College, he wrote the following:

> As I engage in the so-called "bull sessions" around and about the school, I too often find that most college men have a misconception of the purpose of education. Most of the "brethren" think that education should equip them with the proper instruments of exploitation so that they can forever trample over the masses. Still others think that education should furnish them with noble ends rather than means to an end.
>
> It seems to me that education has a two-fold function to perform in the life of man and in society: the one is utility and the other is culture. Education must enable a man to become more efficient, to achieve with increasing facility the legitimate goals of his life.
>
> Education must also train one for quick, resolute and

effective thinking. To think incisively and to think for one's self is very difficult. We are prone to let our mental life become invaded by legions of half truths, prejudices, and propaganda. At this point, I often wonder whether or not education is fulfilling its purpose. A great majority of the so-called educated people do not think logically and scientifically. Even the press, the classroom, the platform, and the pulpit in many instances do not give us objective and unbiased truths. To save man from the morass of propaganda, in my opinion, is one of the chief aims of education. Education must enable one to sift and weigh evidence, to discern the true from the false, the real from the unreal, and the facts from the fiction...

...If we are not careful, our colleges will produce a group of close-minded, unscientific, illogical propagandists, consumed with immoral acts. Be careful, "brethren!" Be careful, teachers! *

If we really examine society today and look at the deeds and acts of those we call "educated," it would seem that King predicted the future. Examine the crimes of Wall Street — the raiding of pension funds or the outsourcing of jobs to simply boost profits. Recall Worldcom, Enron, Tyco, Martha Stewart, and Sam Waksal. Examine these so-called educated people and the institutions they created. Look closely at what we find in their wake.

My father believes that an education should allow you to fend for yourself by preparing you to provide a service. His entrepreneurial mental-

---

* Quoted from an article King wrote for the Morehouse College Campus newspaper, *The Maroon Tiger,* vol. 10, January-February 1947.

ity carried him to where he is today, so he always asks, "What are you doing for yourself?" He believes that an individual should control his or her own destiny.

Create something every consumer will want and don't allow anyone to dictate your future. As the world shifts to a knowledge-based economy, we must stand on our own. We often hear politicians say they're concerned about the outsourcing of jobs overseas, because it produces communities continuously decimated by the loss of high-paying skill jobs and the overabundance of low-paying service jobs. By focusing on developing transferable skills, individuals can define their own futures and protect themselves from the ups and downs of the job market.

Continue to look for the opportunity to serve other individuals, and at the end of the day, you'll create opportunity rather than waiting for someone to do it for you. My father saw his opportunity in roofing and, by pursuing it, managed to free himself from his dependency on the cotton fields. Many individuals today are working for corporations and don't see the opportunity to provide a service to other companies. They settle, working for others instead of working for themselves. We should all seek to infuse a little bit of the entrepreneurial spirit in us, because it's this spirit that spurs us on to make things happen for ourselves.

After all, the promise of America is freedom, and we must use this freedom to chart our own futures regardless of our level of education. Every day each of us should awake and seek to serve humankind in some shape, form, or fashion, because in a capitalist system, you'll be rewarded or paid for your services. Whether you're offering your mind, back, or hands, America is full of opportunity for the individual willing to package his or her services.

Working through college, I was certain that I would make it in this world regardless of whether I finished my degree or not. I knew as long as there is a God and four seasons I'd be able to survive and provide for my family and myself, because I'd mow your lawn, wash your car, paint your house, or repair your roof, no matter what. Manual labor was not, and is not, beneath me.

Formal vs. real education

Understanding that college isn't for everyone, the definition of education must be broad enough for training that doesn't include college.

My father succeeded by learning a skill and serving people. We must similarly teach skill training in our society.

Society needs very formally educated people, but we also need people who can actually do things like build, repair, and service. If you don't think this kind of training is very profitable, just wait until you get a house and something happens with your plumbing. You'll call a plumber, and as soon as he starts giving you his price quotes, I bet you'll say or think, "Man, I should have gone to plumbing school." I know I've expressed this thought a million times.

In discussing the differences between formal and real education, I'm reminded of the story about two men, Mr. Degree and Mr. Trade. An upscale hotel was seeking an operational manager and these guys, Mr. Trade and Mr. Degree, were the last two people to interview for the position. Mr. Trade entered first, introduced himself, and said, "Hi, I'm Mr. Trade and I've had operational management jobs at different hotels. I was successful and went beyond what was required of me. I think I can come into your hotel and do all that is required. I can balance the books and, more importantly, I can work with my hands. I can fix things and save additional money."

Interested, the interviewer responded, "You know Mr. Trade, I think you're the man for the job, but I have one other person to interview. As a matter of fact, how about you just sit outside and we will interview him and make the decision today?" Mr. Trade said, "okay" and took a seat in the reception area outside of the office.

The next guy, Mr. Degree, entered the room and said, "Hi, my name is Mr. Degree. I have a Bachelor of Science degree from Morehouse College, a M.B.A. from Harvard Business School, and I've spent five years on Wall Street. I've managed some of the biggest firms up and down this country. I don't work with my hands but if anything breaks, I know how to develop a request for proposals, accept bids, analyze them, and complete the entire job at the lowest, cheapest cost, thus saving money. I even know how to grow the business and maybe expand this hotel into a convention center, creating additional lines of revenue." The intrigued and excited interviewer said, "You're the man for the job. Let's go outside and tell Mr. Trade that he's qualified but things just didn't work out this time."

They both went out to the reception area where Mr. Trade was waiting and the interviewer introduced Mr. Trade to Mr. Degree and said, "Mr. Trade, with all due respect, you're very well qualified for this job, but we think Mr. Degree will serve us better." Mr. Trade replied, "Well, thank you for the consideration and opportunity to interview," and he left the hotel.

Mr. Trade headed off from the hotel walking down the busy street. He was hungry and only had a dollar in his pocket, but he saw a man on the sidewalk selling apples two for a dollar. He approached the man and purchased two apples. He ate one and walked about a mile with

29

the extra apple in his hand. He had this additional apple and realized he really didn't need it, so he wrote "$2" on it and stood at a traffic light. Someone passed by in his car and asked, "How much is that apple?" and Mr. Trade responded, "Two dollars." The man said, "okay," pulled out his wallet, gave Mr. Trade the money, and drove off. Mr. Trade with two dollars in hand and the wheels of his mind churning said, "Wait a minute." He walked back a mile and bought four more apples with the two dollars he had, returned to the spot where he sold his first apple, and wrote "$2" on all the apples he just bought. In less than an hour, he sold them all and made eight dollars. "I'm definitely on to something," Mr. Trade thought to himself. Then he walked back down a mile, bought a crate of apples, sat them down on his corner, and sold them all by the end of the day.

Eventually, Mr. Trade owned and operated a little fruit stand in the middle of the block. When he had saved enough money selling fruit, he opened his own store on the corner. Ultimately, Mr. Trade expanded his store into a supermarket a block long.

One day this very professionally dressed person entered the store and took his time looking around and collecting a few groceries in a basket. Mr. Trade was busy mopping and cleaning his store when this business-person walked by him and almost slipped! Mr. Trade, protecting his investment and the guy's health, grabbed the man by the jacket, breaking his fall, and told him, "Please sir, watch your step, we wouldn't want you to fall." The business guy, recapturing his composure, said, "Thank you, sir" and was about to go back to shopping when he stopped for a second and looked Mr. Trade straight in the face. "Don't I know you?" the businessman asked. Mr. Trade immediately responded saying, "You do look familiar." "Oh, I know where I recognize you from," the businessman said, "You and I interviewed together for that job at the hotel some time ago." Mr. Trade smiled and said, "That's right, you're Mr. Degree." Mr. Degree, eager to tell him what he was doing, stated, "You know, I'm now the head manager at the hotel. I oversee the entire place. I oversee catering, the convention center, the hotel, and housekeeping, all of that. 500 people answer to me." Mr. Trade happily listening said, "That's nice, good for you."

Mr. Degree then asked, "Well, what do you do?" Mr. Trade replied, "This is my place." "You mean you work here?" "No," Mr. Trade said, "This is my place." "You manage this store?" "No, this is my place, I own it." Impressed, Mr. Degree said, "You own this store? Wow, just think where you'd be if you had my education." Mr. Trade responded bluntly, "Down there. Managing that hotel."

Mr. Trade understood, much like the poet John Keats, that education is not the filling of a bucket, but the lighting of a fire. When you're educated you're supposed to be in the position to do whatever you choose. If you want to work for somebody, go work for somebody, but always keep your independence. There may be a time or day your boss comes to you and says you're no longer needed because the company has to downsize. That's when you should be able to say, "Oh yeah, well I downsized you yesterday because I'm educated, I'm degreed, I have my training, and I can do whatever I want to do."

My father has been a self-employed businessman for 40 years. I used to work for him when I was a little kid and sat at his knee learning to bend and shape gutters. The evening would be rapidly approaching, darkness encroaching upon us, and I'd say, "Dad, let's go home." "Boy, what I'm doing is for me," he'd reply. "We don't stop working until we can't see anymore. One day you're going to understand."

Today, I do understand. Society has made education a swap meet. You pay an institution some tuition; the institution in turn gives you a piece of paper to take somewhere else and swap off. You're allowed to hang your degree on a wall, show up every day, and perform your tasks. When the clock strikes five o'clock, you clean your desk and head home not realizing that your destiny and future are in someone else's hands. An education is supposed to set you free and set you on fire. Every day, regardless of where you hang your degree, your mind should be focused on creating value and worth. Outsourcing or layoffs don't worry you because you know you have skills, training, and education, and these things permit you to create opportunity outside of a company.

My father's training has prepared me for the 21st century where all employees are free agents. Tomorrow is not guaranteed to anyone, and for that reason, you should spend every single day increasing your knowledge and skill set. Mr. Trade would have been very happy working at the respectable hotel, but when that dream didn't materialize he had to make a way in the world with the knowledge he possessed. Mr. Trade is no better or greater than Mr. Degree; he simply didn't accept what the world had presented to him. Instead, he looked for opportunity within himself and his life. As the world continues to change, many individuals will find themselves in Mr. Trade's position, and they will either make do or die.

Three Steps for Enhancing Your Education

Our education, training, and experience encompass all of the tools and mechanisms we need in order to be creative, productive, and successful in this world. There's no magic pill for receiving an education and training. You grow by doing. Getting up every day and committing to learning and mastering something is the only way we gain formal or real life education. Many individuals are waiting for someone to hit them in the head with a book, but education doesn't happen through osmosis. After deciding what your service to society or your craft will be, you must commit to growing in that area.

· ·

"The educated of the 21st century will be he or
she who can learn, unlearn and relearn."

– Alvin Toffler

· ·

The author and futurist Alvin Toffler gave us three steps everyone can take to enhance their education in the 21st century: learn, unlearn, and relearn.*

1 Learn

Commit to understanding what talent or skills you possess to serve society. Take whatever courses or training necessary to improve yourself and better serve others. In America, you receive payment for what you know, and pay for what you don't know. At the end of the day, it's imperative that everyone knows some marketable skill, task, or transferable knowledge in order to survive. Commit to lifelong learning or suffer the consequences — for there is no education or set of skills that will sustain you forever into the future.

In 1990 when I began graduate school in the mechanical engineering department at Georgia Tech, I'd never heard the words "email," "Pentium," "web site," or "Internet." Six years later, after obtaining my doctoral degree, I was emailing people around the world, seeking employment on the Internet, and creating my own web site that

---

* Alvin Toffler. *Future Shock*. New York: Random House, 1970. p. 31.

chronicled my sojourn through graduate school. My learning curve in the area of technology continues to climb straight up.

Presently at the start of the 21st century, we're being bombarded with new rapidly developing technologies that will profoundly affect and transform all of our lives, and create new opportunities for employment. The new opportunities are primarily concentrated in the areas of nanotechnology, biotechnology, information technology, or the convergence of all three. These industries will continue to seek and attract highly educated, trained, and motivated individuals focused on developing technologies. Although my doctorate is concentrated in fluid mechanics, I'm presently learning about the convergence of these three technologies so I can update my knowledge and continue to participate in my profession.

All of us must commit to lifelong continuous learning or risk being left behind. For me, this means learning new technology with new nomenclature and definitions. What are you learning today that will allow you to participate in your profession tomorrow?

2 Unlearn

We must become proficient at noticing the trends of the marketplace and the world. I would've hated to have been the last person selling horse saddles and whips when Henry Ford created the Model T. It's frightening, but technology and growth have the ability to render us or our businesses obsolete in a flash.

I watched Home Depots pop up all around the city of New Orleans while my father was still selling roofing material. Like the famous dime store, Woolworth, and the retailer, Sears, my father's company didn't foresee the impact Walmart would have on their business model. Each suffered the consequences of not unlearning the known and routine and then adopting the new way of doing things. Home Depot was selling roofing material at a price my father's supply business couldn't beat, but he still refused to unlearn and adapt. Eventually the roofing supply business closed down, defeated by progress and change.

"The most potent weapon of the oppressor, is the mind of the oppressed."

– Steven Biko,
South African anti-Apartheid activist

By nature, people usually resist change. They prefer the familiar, old, comfortable ways of doing things. I have an uncle who still has a rotary phone because he refuses to grow into the future. There are phones on the market now that will dial a person's number for you just by saying his or her name, but here's my uncle dialing the old-fashioned way, one finger at a time. The rotary phone is the only phone he knows, and it's the only phone he ever will know, because he doesn't want to unlearn the past.

But consider where America would be if we didn't unlearn some of the policies of the past. Remember, women were once expected to marry by 20, stay home, and raise the children. Women and blacks weren't allowed to vote. Blacks were treated as second-class citizens and counted as 3/5ths of a person. Men didn't go to the doctor, and the doctors were all men. Many corporations and educational institutions were open to white Anglo Saxon Protestant males only, and Native Americans were thought to be uncivilized savages who needed to be exterminated. Society as a whole had to unlearn these biases and prejudices in order to move forward, and thank God, they now only belong in our past.

Still today we must commit to unlearning the beliefs and knowledge of the past because they continue to serve as impediments to moving forward into the future. There are still places in Asia where baby girls are murdered at birth. In some African countries the circumcision of women is still practiced and condoned. America and Europe still horde food when millions of children starve worldwide. As the world grows technically, it's my hope that it will also grow humanely. By unlearning the past we don't forget the past; we simply refuse to move forward with those things we now know to be wrong, inhumane, and painful.

My uncle with his rotary phone may be happy to live in the Dark Ages, but we should expect a more enlightened perspective from each other. Unlearn some of the obsolete past and commit to learning a new paradigm every day in order to live and to grow.

3 Relearn

A day will come when your knowledge base will become obsolete and you'll have to unlearn what you know and then relearn something totally different in order to participate in the economy and marketplace.

Whether we've attended college, trade school, or learned from experience, we must eventually relearn additional information and skills. The world and technology are changing too rapidly to think that we know enough in this lifetime. Critical thinking skills are so important because they allow us to see what's coming in the future and adequately prepare for it. Today, my father's roofing business is called Mackie Roofing and Home Improvement. To survive, he has had to close the roofing supply portion of the company that became unfeasible due to Home Depot, expand his offerings, and learn something he didn't know before. Roofing technology has evolved so much that he has had to unlearn some old techniques and replace them with new ones in order to compete.

My father has always prided himself on beating anyone with a hammer when nailing asphalt fiberglass shingles. In the mornings, he would get on one end of the roof with one helper and he would order all of us to start at the other end. It was absolutely amazing to watch him with a hammer and a nail bag. He'd grab a handful of nails and just start hammering, with each nail automatically falling perfectly between his fingers as he grabbed them from the bag. Without straightening his back out once from his crouched position, he'd nail more shingles than an entire group of men. He showed us what "manpower" really meant.

In the past few years, however, technology has developed a compressed air-powered nail gun that only requires a man to follow a line and press a button. Machines are the equivalent of slave labor. They're cost-effective and cheap, and anyone who tries to compete with slave labor will lose. My father couldn't compete with the air gun, so eventually he learned how to use it. In essence, he had to relearn his craft or lose to the new technology.

Likewise, the integration and synergy of today's multiple technologies will continue to give rise to new and exciting technological markets. We must seek to develop a fundamental understanding of the basic science and physics behind these developing technologies if we expect to be truly educated in the 21st century.

WILLIE'S VIEW

It wasn't by accident that I graduated from college. It wasn't even an option in my life. Other students I graduated from high school with were thinking at the end of the year about what they were going to do. Not me. I was thinking about leaving to go to college.

My educational experience was very different from others. Not one time after elementary school did my parents tell me to go for a degree, or try to influence me in any way about my choice of school. Believe it or not, that decision was totally up to me.

I know the driving force in my education was listening to my dad talk about his educational experience. I'd sometimes listen to the stories he told about how far he had to walk in the cold weather to get to school, the two pair of pants and one shirt that were the only clothes he had to put on his back, and the lack of formal teaching he received. Somehow his stories just stuck to me and influenced me to take advantage of the opportunities he didn't have and go on as high as I could in school.

After all those stories about his lack of education and frustration with the whole thing, I never knew my dad cared about school. My dad wasn't the type to go to my school for conferences or parent events. He left all that stuff up to my mom. He'd just come home and get a report of what was going on and if something was wrong, he'd get dreadfully upset.

I was very excited when I learned that I was going to graduate from high school. That same day I was nominated for the American Legion Award. The winner would be announced at graduation. I rushed home and told my family and waited in great anticipation to tell my dad.

Later that evening when he arrived back from work I rushed to tell him about the award. He seemed unmoved about my celebratory news and I was so disappointed that I went outside and stayed out most of the evening. I got to thinking, and it hit me: My dad has never been to school to see anything I did. Is he even coming to graduation? I went to my mom and told her what I'd been thinking and she said I was crazy for even thinking it. "The problem is," she told me, "you're too much like your dad and you're trying to prove something to him. Your dad will be there." But the uneasy look she had didn't exactly sell me. To make it worse, my graduation was on a workday and my father never, ever missed work. Not once.

Graduation came and we assembled on that huge stage facing the audience like we were all on trial. I looked all over the auditorium, trying to find my family, but the bright lights blocked my vision. I was terrified and didn't know why. Then the moment came in the program when the superintendent stood up to announce the winner of the American Legion Award. He walked to the microphone and said all the stuff you never listen to at a graduation. All I wanted him to do was call my name for that award. I was so distracted, worrying about whether he'd call it or not, that I missed it. The entire class stood and applauded me and I just stood there applauding with them. The girl next to me hit me in the side and said, "Go ahead, dummy, go ahead!" I just stared at her in disbelief.

Walking to that podium with the entire auditorium cheering for me made me feel like I was King of the World.

When I received the award, the superintendent put his arms around me and turned me to the audience. The applause became increasingly loud. I looked all over for my mom and my Aunt Francis. I couldn't find them right away, but I saw another figure in the audience, a slim dark-shaded man with a half-grin on his face and his hands behind his back as if an army sergeant had put him at rest. I couldn't believe it. That was Willie Mackie Sr., taking time out of a workday to finally come see me at school. My smile was so big I felt my jaw muscles ache. I waved ecstatically at him and my family.

After graduation I met my family outside for my hugs and gratuities. My dad pulled me on the side and told me this: "Boy, in my life I've been very successful. I've built my company from my bare hands. I've given you children everything you ever could want. I've taken care of your mother the best I know how and I did it with half of an education. If I could do all this and not have an education, just imagine what you'll do with what you've got." He slapped me on the shoulder and said "Aight boy," which, for all you who don't speak Willie Mackie Sr., means "good job." Then he looked at me and said, "You'll be a boy to me 'til the day I die."

40

At that moment it became very clear to me that my education had to continue. It was like my dad was trying to give me a message but couldn't say it in clear words. He gave me that half-grin, and a hundred bucks I might add, said his goodbyes, and left to go back to work. I just stood there and watched him leave and knew in my heart that he'd just challenged me to continue my education.

Learn to Love What You Do or Find Something Else to Do

Roofing 101

On a bright and sunny day, I stepped outside and saw my neighbor on his roof. He had been up there for the past three straight weekends trying to find and fix a leak. I walked over and chatted with him from the ground while he serviced the roof. Noticing the perspiration dripping off his burnt face, I told him of my days when I had to climb on roofs with my father, and we laughed about how dirty, hard, and difficult the roofing profession was.

Later that day, my father unexpectedly dropped over to my house for one of his five-minute visits. As he pulled into the driveway, he instantly noticed my neighbor working on the roof. He exited his truck without ever looking toward my house. His eyes were riveted on that roof. I walked over to his truck and said hello. "Calvin," he asked without missing a beat, "do you know that guy on the roof over there?" "Yeah, that's my neighbor Roger," I responded.

Calvin and his father in Pontiac, MI on summer vacation in 1977.

Willie Sr. and Anthony at sister Linda's wedding in 1982.

Calvin graduates from Georgia Tech in
September, 1990 with a Bachelor's degree in
mechanical engineering.

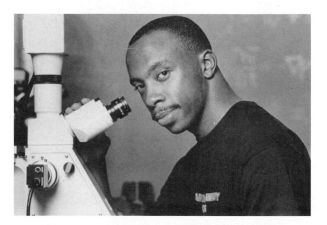

Calvin does research towards his Ph.D. degree at Georgia Tech.

Calvin heads for the gym as a freshman at
Morehouse College.

The Mackie Brothers put on their Annual Christmas Concert.

The Mackie Brothers attend a Mardi Gras Ball
in New Orleans in 1995.

Anthony's headshot, which has landed him in Gap & GQ ads.
(photo by Chia Messina)

Willie Jr.

Calvin and Anthony celebrate Anthony's graduation from Juilliard in May 2001.

Calvin and wife, Tracy, celebrating Life & Love.

Calvin animatedly presents for the DuPont
Corporation's MLK Day Educational
Convocation in Wilmington, DE.

Crouching Tiger, Hidden Dragon: Calvin seriously emphasizes a point during a keynote.

Willie Mackie standing in front of the warehouse he built nearly 30 years ago.

Calvin accepts the 2003 Presidential Award
for Excellence in Science, Mathematics and
Engineering Mentoring at the White House.

The Mackie Men celebrating Christmas 2003 with the newest
addition – Calvin's son, Myles Amad.

Before I could say another word, he began walking toward Roger's house. I could see where this was headed. I pleaded for him to turn around and come back, but he was a determined man.

My father called out to Roger, who had returned to his hammering, and asked him what he was doing. Roger smiled and told him he had a leak in the roof that he was trying to fix. My father told him that he was a roofer and asked if he could take a look. Roger climbed down the ladder, shook his hand, introduced himself, and said, "Sure, be my guest."

My father, dressed in a golf shirt and tennis shorts, climbed up the ladder like a kid just granted permission to enter the McDonald's playground. He canvassed the roof inspecting the work. Without looking at us, he extended his open hand and asked for a hammer. He then began to rip up the shingles and plaster Roger had spent all weekend putting into place! Roger looked like he was going to cry.

Before I could apologize, my dad told Roger to come up the ladder. In an instant, he began to teach a class I had seen many times over on those hot summer days as a kid: Roofing 101. He found the original location of the leak, which Roger and his friend had misdiagnosed, and explained why Roger's effort would only exacerbate the problem rather than fix it. He then demonstrated what needed to be done to solve the problem and started the initial work to get them going in the right direction.

My father told me to go get two tubes of sealant from the rear of his truck. He then gave the tubes to Roger with instructions that he spread this sealant liberally over the affected area. This entire crash course in roofing transpired in 20 minutes under a hot summer sun, and it was an amazing spectacle to watch. My father had tar all over his hands, dirt on his shorts, and a smile on his face. He was on the job and loving every minute of it. My neighbor offered him a beer and money for the material, but my father wouldn't have any of it. "It's my pleasure," he said, and I knew he meant it.

In essence, roofing is something my father would do for free. He loves it. However, it wasn't always this way.

My father arrived in New Orleans with 25¢ in his pocket and no job. He tried his hand at many things, including being a meat packer and stock clerk at the local supermarket. He was arrested for receiving stolen meat off the back of a delivery truck and spent 48 hours in jail. My father didn't know the meat had been stolen and no one could prove he actually stole it, so the police let him go. On his way out of jail, he decided right then and there that the grocery business was not exactly the right career path for him. But his family didn't have anything to eat and money was tight. He had to find something to do.

The minister who married my father and mother was a roofer and he asked my dad to work with him. What could he say? With no other choice or skills, he soon found himself on the hot black gable rooftops of the long shotgun style houses in New Orleans. Roofing work was just as hard as picking cotton but it was work nevertheless, and it granted him the opportunity to provide for his family. The only problem he had with the job was that the good preacher wouldn't always pay his workers on a consistent basis. Every Friday he gave my father a new creative excuse why he didn't have some or all of the money due to pay him. This was very discouraging for my father because he believes to this day a man is supposed to receive his due for a hard day's work. Regardless, he couldn't quit. A paycheck here and there is better than no paycheck at all, he figured.

Eventually, he obtained enough skills to where he felt comfortable breaking away from the good preacher/bootleg roofer and started out on his own. He didn't have a truck, so he had to place the ladder on his black 1965 Chevrolet. He started out small, getting little repair jobs when he could and doing the best he could all by himself. He had no crew, and often worked well into the night, without eating or stopping for a break. What he didn't know he learned on the job.

That was 40 years ago. Since then, he has toiled and sweated on those hot roofs every day to place food on the table and put his kids through college.

> *"Forget about likes and dislikes. They are of no consequence. Just do what must be done. This may not be happiness, but it is greatness."*
>
> – George Bernard Shaw

My father probably didn't grow up dreaming about becoming a roofer, but working in the hot sun and humid summers of Louisiana pulling cotton from the burnt red clay didn't exactly provide a vision of life that included a white shirt and corner office.

It's obvious now that he loves roofing and there isn't much anyone can teach him about it. We've never really sat down and talked about whether or not he enjoyed being a roofer at the very beginning of his life. In truth, he really didn't have much of a choice. My father did what he had to do at the time for his family and learned to love his work along the way, simply because life didn't present him with many other options. It wasn't until much later in his life, after he had mastered his trade and made it his own, that he began to like his profession. What made roofing a dream job for him was his willingness to invest his whole life and energy into becoming the best roofer he could be, and maybe the best roofer in all of New Orleans.

To this day, I don't believe my father ever discovered his true life's purpose. But I do believe it discovered him.

Do What Has to Be Done and You May Find Your True Talent to Transform an Industry, Maybe Even the World

All of us possess some genius. However, most of us spend a lifetime never truly tapping into our true potential for many reasons. Whether we've found our true purpose or not, we should do everything to the best of our abilities and make an effort to do it like no other man or woman living would do it. If we do this, in the end, we'll make it in this world, especially in America, where I truly believe anyone can become great.

As was the case with my father, circumstances beyond our control usually determine what many of us eventually do in our lives. They don't allow us the freedom and opportunity to examine and explore our true calling as ordained by our creator. In America, everyone is born equally, but everyone is definitely not born equal.

The current President of the United States, George W. Bush, was born into a situation that has helped him become the leader of the Free World. He and I came into existence through the same process and procedure, which included a gush of blood, water, pain, and the severing of an umbilical cord. When we both departed the hospital, however, we were greeted by very different limits, constraints, and circumstances. In essence, we were physically born into one common country, but socially born into two different worlds.

Supported by the wealth and influence of his parents and family lineage, which can be traced all the way back to the first wealthy merchants of this country, "George W." had ample time to explore and ponder life and determine what he wanted to contribute to this world. Yale, Harvard, and other Ivy League institutions were par for his course. He was able to vacation anywhere in the world, rub shoulders with elite and prestigious people, and gain access to opportunities a common man such as my father — his contemporary — never even knew existed. So, how does one compete with such a scenario?

The truth is we must realize that we're not competing against anything but our own potentials. George W. Bush's situation is not one any person could create or discover. He was born into his situation, just like you and I are born into ours. His situation was created by ancestors who capitalized on the opportunities presented to them at the time. Therefore, everyone must start where they can and capitalize on the unique opportunities before them. My father saw his opportunity in roofing and he has continuously developed this talent into genius. Roofing may not have been his true calling and purpose, but he took the opportunity to turn it into something very special and profitable for him.

All of us have the ability to transform our lives into something very special, special in the sense that generations from now people will know your name, and your work will be so great generations yet unborn will study your life's undertakings and accomplishments.

Talent does not necessarily equal purpose

When I entered college, it was clear I knew and understood mathematics at a level beyond the average college student, so naturally I chose math as my major concentration area. I never thought to ask myself whether this was my purpose and my gift, I only knew I was good at it, and everybody assumed it was what I was supposed to be doing with my life. Since then I have toiled in mathematics and engineering and made a decent living in such toils, but it's also clear to me now that my real gift is teaching, and not necessarily the study and application of math, science, and engineering alone. I have come to like the math, science, and engineering, but I am now nurturing the teacher in me — the person who can reach individuals at different places in their consciousness and development. Pursuing what I had talent in has helped me discover my true gift, if not on purpose, then by accident.

The reason so many young people today are in careers and professions they absolutely hate is because people guided them there based on their ability to perform in the area. These people meant well, but they were mistaken. They assumed that talent equaled purpose in life. Like my father, these misled young people face a decision: change their current profession or career path for one more suited to their true callings, or commit to transforming their profession into something they like and love by understanding how they're serving and contributing to society. My father didn't have the luxury of changing his career path, but it might not be too late for some of us.

Seeking your true purpose

A good place to start in seeking your true purpose, talent, and genius is by asking yourself two questions: "What do I like doing?" and "What would I do for free?" Many of us spend a lifetime laboring in tasks we hate. If you awake every day and arrive to a place or job you hate, you definitely won't reach your true potential. Attitude plays a large role in determining what you like or dislike.

Like and dislike don't matter in my world. I look at what needs to be accomplished in order to get me where I want to be. I may not know where I want to be in ten years, but while I'm working in my present position, I'm definitely looking toward the future. Maybe my father hated roofing, the heat, humidity, and labor. Maybe he walked up to the roof and said to himself, "I have no choice, I have to make this work. I have no other skills or opportunities so I have to create them for myself." All I know for certain is that my father loves what he does today and no man living or yet born will ever approach a roof with the zeal and zest he demonstrates every day. Sometimes it's the situations where we are most miserable that bring out the best in us.

If you know what you like doing, your goal should be to do that for a living. If you enjoy doing it, you'll probably do it better than someone who hates it or has a bad attitude about doing it. Who ever thought Martha Stewart could create a billion dollar business in the lifestyle industry, making homemaking cool and acceptable? She loved designing and decorating and pursued it as a living and a career. There was no model in her field for excellence, so she created the model. Many of us spend weekend hours on hobbies that otherwise can be careers in a free society. Do what you enjoy doing or make the best of what you're doing now while you're doing it.

You often hear athletes say they'd play their sport every day even if they had to do it for free. They absolutely love what they're doing. I'm convinced that all of us have that kind of passion for something in our lives.

Some of the greatest technological advancements of the digital revolution at the turn of the 21st century resulted from individuals doing what they loved. Many tools and mechanisms created were originally designed to solve technical issues that would make the everyday life of these designers, inventors, and engineers easier. In the process of doing what they enjoyed and would perform for free, they created billion dollar corporations and hundreds of thousands of jobs. This country has witnessed the greatest wealth creation in the history of the world because of people doing nothing more than what they loved.

I remember getting on the cumbersome Internet in the early 1990s and going to the University of Illinois web site to download a program called Mosaic. Mosaic was a tool created by graduate students at the university to help students readily navigate the Internet, which at that time was a place where "techies" met and transported code and other technical information. "Internet" wasn't even a household word. Eventually, Mosaic became what we presently call Netscape and when the company that invented it entered the public stock market it had the largest stock price increase in one day for a company in the history of Wall Street at that time. The Netscape Initial Public Offering (IPO) of stock launched the technology bubble. Marc Andreessen and his friends were only doing what they loved when they created Mosaic, but they eventually changed the world and the way we do business.

David Filo and Jerry Yang were graduate students at Stanford who loved to drink Yoohoo milk and tinker on the Internet at all hours of the night.

Graduate students over the country really loved the Internet because they could email people and friends all over the country and rapidly find information they'd otherwise have to find though hours of research in the library. Someone could instantly send a FTP (File Transfer Program) to another person's server that would otherwise take days via regular snail mail. However, the Internet was haphazardly and cumbersomely organized. As more people created web sites, it became increasingly more difficult to find their locations. Yang and Filo created a directory of sites and began to catalog locations. You could go to their site and find universities, research labs, and other sites otherwise lost in cyberspace. We know the rest of the story, as their YAHOO! directory has become one of the greatest successes of the Internet age. Two graduate students attempted to solve their personal dissatisfaction with Internet chaos and wound up changing the world.

All of us have the ability to change the world, maybe not on the scale of a YAHOO! or Netscape; but when you attempt to apply your talents toward some issue for free, just for the sake of improving humankind or our existence on earth, you open up the universe for your use. These individuals weren't seeking money, but they became tremendously wealthy doing what they knew and loved.

The transformation: giving meaning to your work

As mentioned previously, there are many obstacles that keep us from pursuing our true purpose in life. For my father, those obstacles were his lack of education and desperation for a job — any job at all. Today, he loves his job and has learned to love his work by giving it more meaning, seeking ways to serve others and achieve excellence.

Perhaps you don't have the luxury at this point in time to quit your current career path in hopes of finding your true purpose. That's okay; as my father's story exemplifies, sometimes we stumble upon our true calling simply by accident, or sometimes we make a career path our true path by learning to view it from a different perspective. Start where you are by transforming your attitude about what you're doing now because it may provide you with the avenue to determine and pursue your true calling.

We begin to transform our lives and our careers when we ask a simple question: "How can I serve?" or "How can I help?" In doing this, we remove the focus from what we want and place it on serving humanity. Our attitudes begin to change and we see our situation from a different perspective. Instead of coming to work lamenting our position and job, we begin to seek out the ways in which people are served and transformed by our job. Our profession and task take on a very divine purpose because now we're participants in developing a better world.

My wife may hate being a pharmacist, the long hours, no lunch break, no downtime, cantankerous customers, and the fast food pharmaceutical retail business model. However, when she begins to talk about her customers from the perspective of the prescription she filled, or the counseling she provided, an entirely different attitude emanates from her voice. She understands that the tasks she performs and the information she shares are helping people and that she is serving the universe through her knowledge. When a worried mother comes in to acquire a prescription for her sick child, her attitude is really adjusted. Those are the days she loves her work and looks forward to the next day.

I know there were days when my father didn't want to climb up on a hot roof, but by asking himself how his work served others, he created strength and motivation for himself. He'd realize his efforts protected a family from the threatening afternoon thundershowers and he'd rise from his bed, ready to hammer down the shingles. When we take our wants, our personalities, and our egos out of the equation and ask simply, "How can I serve?" the answer is readily presented. Our lives and work take on newfound meaning regardless of whether we're operating within our God-given purpose. A spiritual and mental transformation takes place and we immediately begin to love what we do.

Once we have come to love what we do, the next step is to seek the things we were placed on this earth to do. Former President Jimmy Carter sought to help the world become a better place by becoming the President of the United States. Since serving as a one-term president, he has spent his remaining life serving people all around the world. Maybe the Presidency wasn't his true calling or passion but now he's using the experience to do what he believes he was placed on this earth to do.

In essence, we can all begin to love what we do by giving meaning to our work.

Three Ways to Bring More Meaning to Your Work

Your focus in developing your talent and determining your purpose should flow from efforts to serve humankind and help humanity. Therefore, everyone's efforts and works and the subsequent meaning of that work should attempt to address one or more of the three following areas:

1 Serving others to help them grow and develop as human beings

Whenever we put another man's or woman's needs before our own, our actions bring harmony and calming to our spirit. We've been placed on this earth to serve, and in the end, we're supposed to live our lives such that when we die the world will be a better place for the future and our children.

Every day we should awaken and ask ourselves "How can I serve humankind?" We should ask ourselves this because time and history have proven that man and his existence are worth more than just money and material possessions. Great men, rich men, have died and none of their money or material gain saved them or went with them in death. When we leave this earth, the only thing that survives us is the legacy of what we have done for someone else. That's why I believe the greatest profession in the world is that of teaching, because teachers possess the ability to impart a lesson to someone that may one day affect babies yet unborn. As Dr. Martin Luther King Jr. said: "Everybody can be great... because anybody can serve. You don't have to have a college degree to serve. You don't have to make your subject and verb agree to serve. You only need a heart full of grace. A soul generated by love."*

After the tragedy of September 11, 2001, many individuals were on CNN and "Good Morning America" saying that the event served as the impetus motivating them to find purpose in their work. They were frustrated and dismayed that their work was driven by material and monetary greed, and found their lives to be empty. The fact that they had survived 9-11 became an opportunity to do something for someone. The act of serving humankind, feeding the hungry, volunteering at a shelter, working with kids, or donating money to a cause usually brings a sense of satisfaction to even the most cold-hearted individuals.

Determine how your work is transforming lives and you'll find more satisfaction in your life. I remember my father talking about how repairing roofs allowed people to have a comfortable home and come together as a family in the dining room. The pride in his eyes and

---

* Martin Luther King Jr. "The Drum Major Instinct." Delivered at the Ebenezer Baptist Church, Atlanta, Georgia. February 4th, 1968. Published in *A Knock at Midnight: Inspiration from the Great Sermons of Reverend Martin Luther King, Jr.* Clayborne Carson and Peter Holloran, ed.s. New York: IPM/Warner Books, 1998.

power in his voice told me that he knew his work mattered. Your work matters also, just look deep within the monotony and discover how you're serving humankind.

2 Solving problems that prevent people from reaching their potential, and businesses and organizations from operating profitably, effectively, and efficiently

On a trip to Boston, Massachusetts in 1996, I watched as a luggage bin door on a 757 Boeing airliner burst open when the plane landed on the runway at Boston's Logan Airport. Luggage fell from the bin just missing the heads of horrified passengers. This episode wouldn't escape my mind the entire weekend. On returning to New Orleans via the same airline, I became obsessed with the luggage bin, just staring at it and concentrating on it the entire flight. On Monday morning when I entered my office, I began to design a possible solution for this problem.

I couldn't forget the fact that someone might have been hurt by the falling luggage. Research confirmed my fears that there were indeed people who had been seriously injured in such incidents, and that this was an on-going safety issue with other airlines as well. I set to work with a group of students developing a solution, and nearly one year later my students and I received a patent on a device to retrofit luggage stow bins on 737 and 757 Boeing Airliners. We worked day and night to create solutions because we didn't want to see another individual critically injured in an avoidable accident.

The bin solution will serve humankind by protecting people from bodily injury. It will simultaneously help the airline business operate more profitably, effectively, and efficiently. Our work had a purpose and meaning, and every time I get onto an airplane I know that I have participated in an act of service. Even if an airline never purchases or implements the device, I take satisfaction in knowing we created a possible solution.

How does your work serve a business, a community, or humankind? Seek this answer and keep it before you. When you think you're doing meaningless, detached work that only generates profit or makes someone rich, it's easy to lose focus and meaning in your work.

Every day, multi-million dollar deals and decisions are consummated in hotels and conference centers that are maintained and cleaned by individuals who may never see how they played a role in the success of those deals or decisions. If the maid service and maintenance people don't carry out their jobs with pride and purpose, many of those so-called "important deals" wouldn't occur. It's important for corporate leaders to respect the entire food chain of the organizational chart. The accounting scandals that brought down Enron, Lucent, Tyco and WorldCom, destroying people's lives and erasing years of retirement accounts, certainly helped us understand the meaning and purpose of an accountant's work like never before. Many of the accountants who fabricated and distorted profits never attached their work and its meaning to the lives of other employees in the company, and this lack of purpose led to selfish decision-making with devastating results.

Remember, beneath or behind every task, problem, and challenge, there are lives to be saved or enhanced.

3 Promoting and saving causes that benefit humankind

Every year I receive my United Way donation pledge from the dean of my university with a note urging participation. This is a scenario played out all over America. United Way does an excellent job galvanizing people and organizations to help those who are less fortunate. It bothers me, however, that so many individuals have to be prodded to help their fellow man. Many individuals give to the United Way because they don't want to be the only one in the organization who doesn't receive an invitation to the United Way Breakfast. Peer pressure influences adults just as strongly as children.

Serving someone soup on Thanksgiving brings a revelation to you about your life. All of us are one or two unfortunate experiences away from waiting in a soup line. By helping others and charitable organizations, you receive meaning and purpose in your life. Society would be a much better place if everyone were committed to at least one cause that benefited humankind.

As a teacher, I have the opportunity to help individuals develop during a very defining time in their lives. Many of my students upon completing their degrees and getting the "big" jobs return to tell me how unhappy and unsatisfied they are. They talk about the monotony and the detachment of the experience and explain how they expected so much more from life.

I think the emptiness comes from focusing on the job and the task rather than on the benefit and the outcome their jobs have for humankind. They fail to take advantage of the outreach available through their corporations to schools, community groups, and other volunteer activities. They don't consider how they can help the students following them by developing partnerships between their corporation and their alma mater. These are the type of activities that bring satisfaction, meaning, and purpose to a career, to a job, or to life.

WILLIE'S VIEW

I had already decided my career path for college by the time I graduated from high school. After working with my dad all those summers, I quickly realized that the roofing industry just wasn't for me. I actually stopped working with my dad when I became a sophomore in high school and got a job as a dishwasher at a restaurant in the mall. My father was very disappointed at first, but it turned out to be great for me. I worked at the restaurant the three years I was in high school and moved up from position to position very quickly. Each time I moved to another position I got a 5¢ raise. I spent every moment of time away from school at the restaurant because I absolutely loved it. When it was time for me to go away to school, I really started to miss my old job.

When I got to college I started studying law because I'd always dreamed of helping my dad in a way that didn't include backbreaking labor. I just knew I'd picked the career of my life. To make a little extra money I got a job in a local restaurant in the small town where I attended college, and again I got this overwhelming feeling about working in a restaurant I couldn't explain. It was like I was a part of that place. I felt like it was where I belonged. I didn't share this thought with anyone because I knew they'd all think I was crazy. So I just went on studying law in the day and working in the restaurant at night.

Not realizing I was just going through a phase with my education, I decided to change my major from general law to criminal law. Boy! What was I thinking? Things slowly began to get depressing at school. The more I learned about law, the less interested I became.

The final straw came while I was working on my internship my senior year. I got a chance to talk to a guy who was on death row at the state penitentiary. He was in court that day using his last stay of execution to sue his lawyer for misrepresentation. I just couldn't believe I was there talking to a convicted murderer. More so, I couldn't believe that someone was actually hired to represent this man.

Weeks had gone by since I talked to the convict when one day I turned on my television to learn he'd been executed. That was all I could take. I picked up the phone and called my mother and I began to let go on her about the way I was feeling about school and tell her I was coming home. I'd had enough. She talked to me and calmed me down. I heard my dad in the background asking her what I was talking about and when he learned I wanted to come home, he immediately got on the phone. He started his conversation as he always did: "Yeah boy, don't worry about what you're going through, you understand?" Then he lit into me. "You're up there to get an education and that's what you're gonna do. If you don't want to be a lawyer, then don't. But get your degree...I swear to God get your degree." (My father would swear to God about everything.) He gave the phone back to my mom and she continued to talk me down.

After I graduated college I knew I'd never be a lawyer. I actually hated every minute of studying it. I came home and again found myself another job in a local restaurant. This time I was a full manager, and I absolutely loved it. It just seemed as though this career was in me and this was where I should be. Since then I've learned every aspect of the restaurant business and have been very successful in every venture I entered into within that trade.

When you learn the ins and outs of a business, it becomes you. Now when I go out to eat it takes everything in me not to teach and tutor waiters, hosts, cooks, and bartenders. That's the hard part, knowing when to let go.

One night my family decided to give my dad a birthday dinner at the restaurant I managed. I set the whole thing up and it was great. He truly enjoyed himself. Afterwards he came to me and told me how proud he was of me. I'd never heard those words from his lips. I was surprised. After that I thought I could walk on air. I don't think he knows it was the work ethic he instilled in me that made that night so amazing. What a teacher!

Make Self-Discipline Your Habit

The Break Machine

Looking back on my childhood, it's obvious my father didn't know anything about child labor laws, or at least he didn't care about violating them. I don't know at what age I began to follow him to work and carry loads heavier than my body, but I can't remember not going. As a matter of fact, I enjoyed working with my father so much that I gave up summer football practice every year. It wasn't just work to me; it was a labor of love.

At first, I wasn't allowed to go on the roof with the other men. I was what they called a "gofer." "Go get the nails, Calvin," "Go get the hammer," "Go get the water cooler," "Go wash the trucks" — that was all I ever heard for eight to nine hours a day.

· ·

> *"We are what we repeatedly do. Excellence,*
> *then, is not an act, but a habit."*
>
> *– Aristotle*

· ·

61

Then at the age of 11, I learned to drive the forklift at the roofing warehouse. Driving a forklift is different than driving a car because unlike an automobile, the rear wheels turn. This challenge meant nothing to me at the time because I didn't know how to drive a car either. Being a virgin driver actually aided my development; I didn't have any bad habits to unlearn.

I loved to drive the forklift although it was difficult because most of the time you had to drive in reverse while raising or lowering a load attached to the front blades. After learning to drive with some proficiency, I began to unload delivery trucks, which was a very important job. My dad's company was charged for however long the trucks sat — from the time they arrived to the time they were completely empty. The goal was to unload the shingles from the trucks as soon as possible. I devised a plan to unload the trucks as soon as they arrived by placing the loads along the curve in the street. As the trucks departed and the afternoon lull would arrive, I'd begin to move the pallets of material from the street into the warehouse, thus avoiding any overtime charges for the drivers.

I was proud of myself and loved my job, riding the forklift and blowing the horn for people to move. Every day I'd time myself trying to beat the previous time it took for me to remove the shingles from the truck. My dad would marvel at me unloading the truck and yell, "If you damage anything — the truck or the material — you're going to pay for it!" He felt I was too young to be handling so much responsibility, but he gave me the opportunity anyway.

Eventually, my father gave my brother Willie and me more responsibility. Impressed with the progress and growth we made at the warehouse, he had another challenge for us. He moved us inside to the sheet metal shop. Customers at that time were allowed to custom order gutters, down-sprouts, and other roof ornaments, and the sheet metal men were well-trained and made more money than anyone else. My father being a true capitalist figured he could save some money by getting his trusted sons to do some of the work cheaply. He recognized that by training us and having us in the warehouse, the sheet metal men would be able to maximize their time in the field generating revenue and completing jobs.

One particular summer, the company had a big federal government job to repair the roofs on local schools. The job called for custom copper gutters, because copper, although more expensive, was more durable than regular 26-gauge galvanized sheet metal. The government figured they'd pay for quality up front and save money on the backend with diminished maintenance and repair cost.

My father set out to train us on making gutters from scratch. Having received the desired dimensions, we were required to make a master design by tapping dimples into a sheet of metal according to the specifications for the gutters. Once convinced that this was the master, we laid this sheet on top of other sheets one by one and tapped dimples into those sheets. These dimples served as spotters for where the metal needed to be bent on the break machine in order to get the shape of the desired final product.

I still dream about the break machine at night. The machine was a large plate of rustic red steel. The break was a steel table with another steel plate attached above it at a 45-degree angle. The break had a steel-like door attached and swiveled to the front with a large steel weight extending from one end of the door resembling a lever on a Las Vegas slot machine. We would place the metal sheets on the table and lock it down by lowering the 45-degree piece above the table down unto the metal. It was important that the metal was aligned according to the dimples in the master.

With the table and top locked, we would push the steel ball backward raising the steel door on the front of the machine, which would bend the metal. On the end of the machine were degrees engraved in the metal to tell us how far to bend. Sometimes the metal needed 60-degree angles but most of the time the job called for 90-degree bends. My brother and I designed, stamped, and bent metal all day long during the summer. I enjoyed the work but the monotony and repetition almost drove me crazy.

One morning Willie and I had the music going and the sheets of metal flying. Around two o'clock in the afternoon my father came charging into the shop. Working hard and sweating profusely, we ignored him as he stood there staring intently at us while we operated the break machine. Suddenly, he blew his stack and began screaming about the lazy and inconsistent way we were making the metal. He went to his truck and returned with two ten-foot gutters we produced earlier that morning. He laid them on the floor end-to-end with approximately one inch of overlap. He told us to come over and look, and we did. "What do you see?" he asked. Like two little kids, we responded, "Nothing." "Well I see about $10,000 worth of screwed up metal work!" he screamed.

My father pointed out the problems with the metal: The gutters wouldn't sit comfortably within each other, which caused gaps between the metal when the roofers tried to solder them together. Gutters are designed to channel water from the roof to the ground. If gutters have gaps where they connect, they leak and are defective. In our rush to get things done fast, my brother and I had produced some shoddy work and wasted about $10,000 of my father's money.

Needless to say, our father was not happy. He said to us, "You have to become creatures of habit. Discipline yourself to do it right the first time and every time after. Otherwise you'll have to do it all over again and no one's gonna pay you for that." Then he said, screaming almost, "And turn that damn radio off! Get in the habit of coming here and doing your work without all of the horseplay and clowning around. For God's sake, have pride in your work and do it right!"

After our public and humiliating scolding, we immediately began to focus on the quality of our work, not the quantity. We retrained our minds and work habits. We slowed down our pace, and became more conscious of what we were doing and how we were doing it. In the end, our production pace increased again and we mastered making custom metal work efficiently and correctly the first time.

The break machine produced the same results every time. The metal was defective because we approached the machine differently with each sheet. We had to become as consistent as that machine. We had to develop good habits and discipline ourselves to perform the task the same way with each sheet. This is the lesson I learned from that machine and my dad, and I've tried to manifest it in my daily life.

We Have to Become Creatures of Habit in All That We Do

My father is a man of incredible self-discipline. You can set your clock by his schedule. He's up by 6:30 AM, out the door by 7 AM, and at his office by 7:30 AM every day, regardless of the weather or his health.

The warehouse, when it was operational, had to be open by 8 AM and he had to be there, because by that time all of the trucks for the day were loaded and the warehouse was open for business. When 8 AM rolled around during the summers, I'd be sitting on the forklift waiting for the first supply truck to pull around the corner. If we wanted to go to work with daddy during the summers and on the weekends, we had to beat him to his truck. He wouldn't wake us or wait for us. He refused to let our negligence compromise his disciplined approach to work and business.

I remember one Saturday I awoke early to go to work with my father. I lay on the couch downstairs to nap and wait for him to get ready. There was no way he could pass by without seeing me. All he had to do was tap me on his way to the utility room, where he kept his work uniform and shoes, and tell me to wake up.

I woke up an hour later and he had already left for work. When I called him at the warehouse, he made it clear that it wasn't his responsibility to wake me. If I was serious about working, he said, I'd have been awake and on the truck. He explained to me that he had a business to run and men to put on jobs; he didn't have time to play with me and abruptly hung up the phone. I was upset because I looked forward to making my $20 for the four hours of Saturday work. I never again expected my father to wake me for work.

Buddha said that the man who conquers himself is superior to the one who conquers a thousand men in battle. My father conquered his habits a long time ago. He's in control of his daily life and not the other way around. All of us must conquer ourselves by conquering our habits. Habits can either be our companions or our worst enemies.

HABIT

"I am your companion. I am your greatest helper or heaviest burden. I will push you onward or drag you down to failure. I am completely at your command. Half the things you do you might just as well turn over to me and I will be able to do them quickly and correctly. I am easily managed — you must merely be firm with me. Show me exactly how you want something done and after a few lessons I will do it automatically. I am servant of all great men; and alas, of all failures, as well. Those who are great, I have made great. Those who are failures, I have made failures. I am not a machine, though I work with all the precision of a machine plus the intelligence of a man. You may run me for profit or run me for ruin — it makes no difference to me. Take me, train me, be firm with me, and I will place the world at your feet. Be easy with me and I will destroy you.

Who am I? I am habit!"

— Anonymous

We live in a day and age where lack of discipline is the downfall of many people. Words like sacrifice and discipline are almost missing from conversation. People are living from crisis to crisis because they refuse to take control of their lives and live more disciplined in all aspects — financially, spiritually, mentally, and physically. Obesity and heart disease are still the leading causes of death in America, and these ills are the direct results of our inability to discipline and control our wants and desires. As a nation we indulge without restraint and regard for the consequences. Our inability to create and develop good financial habits and discipline leads to unmitigated materialism and consumerism, and these self-defeating habits are now pervasive in the lives of youths as well as adults.

We must commit to changing our bad habits and developing good ones through self-discipline. We must start becoming creatures of habit today, so our good habits can help us lead longer, happier lives. It takes approximately 30 days to establish or break a habit. Commit to mastering one good habit every day and continue to build upon it for the rest your life.

Four Ways to Bring More Discipline to Your Life

There are four main areas, or quadrants, of our lives where we can probably afford to instill more self-discipline. Self-defeating behavior or lack of discipline in these quadrants of life can add additional stress to our lives, and sometimes result in total destruction. When we're experiencing personal problems, we can usually look to these four quadrants for the sources and solutions.

1 The Financial Quadrant

Many people live paycheck-to-paycheck, or worse, a paycheck behind on their bills. This kind of behavior isn't just financially risky, it's also unsatisfying to our creative and spiritual needs as human beings. We can never reach our full potential if we're constantly worried about money or unpaid bills, nor can we ever be truly open and caring to the other people in our lives. Many failed relationships and marriages result from financial difficulties and misunderstandings.

I believe in committing to what I call "The CAN Theory." Make as much money as you CAN, put it in a CAN, and then sit on the CAN! If you CAN do this, then you CAN always have a reservoir of resources to tap into when things get tough. Commit to paying yourself first by saving 10% of everything you earn. For example, I have a habit of never spending my first check. This way, I always have the amount of money I initially made on my job saved and earning interest.

I've always been a frugal shopper and a serious saver. I've never wanted or needed money, though there were some crises that forced me to produce a substantial amount of money without notice. I've always had the last-minute cash I needed stashed away for a rainy day. Since I was a saver, I was able to avoid the stress and pain that comes from not having enough money when it was needed.

I've seen too many families spend money so conspicuously that they're unable to settle family emergencies. They have all the plasma TVs, cigarettes, CDs, DVDs, and leather jackets they could possibly want, but no money to fix the car when it breaks down, or repair the roof when it starts to leak. Parents especially need to be good role models when it comes to financial habits. I learned to be frugal by watching my father, and he learned his good habits from his father before him. Financial discipline creates a lifelong habit which eventually benefits generations yet born, so teach your children to save.

I define being "broke" as spending more than you make. If someone makes one million dollars and spends two million that person is absolutely broke. Many young professionals and entertainers don't understand this simple truism: *A penny saved is definitely a penny earned.* In essence, once you learn and manifest in your life the discipline and habit to save a penny, saving dollars become easier and obvious.

Read books such as Thomas J. Stanley and William D. Danko's *The Millionaire Next Door* (Pocket Books, 1998), and Robert T. Kiyosaki and Sharon L. Lecher's *Rich Dad, Poor Dad* (Warner Business Books, 2001) for introductory lessons on the process of creating financial responsibility and discipline in your life.

2 The Spiritual Quadrant

Anthony de Mello, a Jesuit priest from India, once said: "Spirituality means waking up. Most people, even though they don't know it, are asleep. They're born asleep, they live asleep, they marry in their sleep, they breed children in their sleep, they die in their sleep without ever waking up. They never understand the loveliness and the beauty of this thing that we call human existence."*

Our human existence is first spiritual and must manifest in the physical eventually. All physical realities are first spiritual and mental thoughts. We must take care of our inner self and feel our inner self. Our con-

---

* Anthony de Mello. *Awareness: The Perils and Opportunities of Reality.* New York: Image Books, 1992. p. 5.

sciousness or awareness, which makes us human, must be nurtured and fed.

I have a doctoral degree in mechanical engineering and my area of concentration is in the thermal sciences such as fluid mechanics, heat transfer, and thermodynamics. Thermodynamics gives us the conservation of energy, which we call the first law, and teaches us that the natural tendency of the universe is to degenerate into chaos — a process called entropy. The entropy or disorder of the universe is always increasing, thus our ability to produce is always decreasing. We as humans are in the midst of an always-expanding chaotic universe and, as such, there must be a force or nucleus present to keep us in order. Ultimately, the Creator is the divine force or power that brings order to life.

Spiritual well-being speaks to our ability to tap into this force called the Creator. It's been shown that spiritual people are healthier and happier people as a whole. When you exercise the power that comes from within and tap into the well called the universe, your strength and power become everlasting. You're able to confront forces, evils, and obstacles you never knew you could overcome.

It's our spiritual awareness that promotes unconditional love, respect, and appreciation for life and mankind. It gives us the wisdom and strength to make proper and life-sustaining decisions with respect to everything that is living.

Native Americans and indigenous people have a long history of being one with the universe. I remember as a kid a powerful commercial no longer on American television that usually aired on Saturday mornings in between cartoons such as "Schoolhouse Rock." The commercial showed a Native American perched on a hill overlooking a very polluted river. Powerfully, he would turn his head and look directly into the camera where you'd be able to a see a single tear rolling down his cheek. The image spoke to the spirituality within us, as well as to our oneness with the environment and universe.

Without a spiritual awareness we lose reverence for everything that is life. Without reverence our actions become caustic, rabid, brutal, destructive, abusive, and disrespectful. We wonder what's wrong with the world — terrorism, classism, racism, and sexism — but those "isms" are rooted in the failure to respect and reverence spirituality. When we become reverent, and thus spiritual, we accept and acknowledge that life and everything in it has value. Many individuals address their spiritual needs through prayer, meditation, reading religious books, or practicing a religion of personal choice. We must discipline ourselves not to be spiritually lazy or apathetic and find a way to connect with the Creator in our own lives.

3 The Mental Quadrant

Whenever I think about mental stability, I remember the United Negro College Fund's theme "A Mind is a Terrible Thing to Waste." We have to understand that the brain is a muscle and must be exercised regularly. Illiteracy is rampant in America, a free nation where everyone has the opportunity to receive an education. People are refusing to read, but it's reading, not television, that stimulates the brain.

I've paid a dear price for growing up in a house without books. I've struggled with my reading ability my entire life because I lacked exposure to books and literature as a youngster. When we begin to read our brains respond in absolutely unbelievable ways. That's why we should set some type of annual mental stimulation goal for ourselves, such as reading at least two books a year. Think about it: If you follow this plan, in ten years, you'll have read 20 books. How many other people will be able to say the same thing?

We often look at individuals and think they're brilliant when in reality they've just read what we've refused to read. Personal growth through mental stimulation has to be one quadrant where we spend a lot of time, energy, and resources. Presently, my wife has placed a moratorium on book buying in our household because I try to read everything. Someone once told me you can't know everything. "That's true," I said, "but I can know more every day." Knowing more leaves me with the satisfaction of understanding the world around me.

Illiteracy in America is on the rise and it will have a profound impact on future generations. If we don't want to read for ourselves and develop good mental habits and discipline, then let's do it at least for our children. Research and evidence indicate that mental discipline and stimulation begin not in the schools, but at home. A study conducted by the U.S. Department of Education in 1985 entitled *A Nation at Risk* found that preschool children whose parents read to them are much better prepared to start school and perform significantly better in school than those who haven't been exposed to reading.* Keep that in mind if you want intelligent, critical-thinking kids.

4 The Physical Quadrant

If there's one area of self-discipline in which I've been a colossal failure, this is the one. Over the years, I've always been active and have taken pride in being physically fit. When you take your eyes off your goal of

---

* The National Commission on Excellence in Education. "A Nation At Risk: The Imperative for Educational Reform." Superintendent of Documents. Washington, D.C.: U.S. Government Printing Office, April 1983.

discipline, however, bad habits creep in, sometimes causing bad things to happen.

On an annual routine visit to the doctor last year I discovered I weighed more than ever before. My doctor informed me that I had a very high, potentially dangerous cholesterol level. "Not me," I said. "Yes, you," she retorted, "and if you don't start exercising and eating healthy, you could have a heart attack." Later in the week, I came to terms with the fact that my habits concerning my body were dismal, and I had no one to blame but myself.

The body is a temple and you only have one. Many people presently have debilitating diseases because they didn't focus on the physical quadrant in their lives. I don't want to be one of those people. Physical activity and good nutrition are key factors in leading a healthy lifestyle and reducing chronic illnesses, such as diabetes, obesity, heart disease, colon cancer, and high blood pressure.

The Centers for Disease Control (CDC) has given us simple ways to increase physical activity in our daily lives. By modifying the activities we do every day, we can burn off some of the calories that add up during the day while we do nothing but sit on our butts and type away at our desks.

Some simple modifications include:*

- Walking, cycling, jogging, skating, etc., to work, school, the store, or place of worship.
- Parking the car farther away from your destination.

---

* Taken from the Centers for Disease Control web site, www.cdc.gov.

- Getting on or off the bus several blocks away.
- Taking the stairs instead of the elevator or escalator.
- Playing with children or pets. (Everybody wins. If you find it too difficult to be active after work, try it before work.)
- Taking fitness breaks, walking or doing desk exercises, instead of taking cigarette or coffee breaks.
- Performing gardening or home repair activities.
- Avoiding labor saving devices. (Turn off the self-propel option on your lawn mower or vacuum cleaner.)
- Using leg power. (Take small trips on foot to get your body moving.)
- Exercising while watching TV. (For example, use hand weights, stationary bicycle/treadmill/stair climber, or stretch.)
- Dancing to music.
- Keeping a pair of comfortable walking or running shoes in your car and office. (You'll be ready for activity wherever you go!)
- Making a Saturday morning walk a group habit.
- Walking while doing errands.

With a little creativity and planning, even the busiest people in the world can make room for more physical activity in their day. Simply put, there's no excuse for why we all shouldn't develop more discipline in this quadrant!

WILLIE'S VIEW

When my brother and I arrived for work each morning, we never knew what my dad had planned for us. It was no secret that we were the hired help. One morning my dad started a job at the Coca-Cola plant located just blocks away from the warehouse. I was told that morning that I'd be on the crew to get that job going. What it really meant was that I'd be one of the guys tearing up the roof.

The Coca-Cola job was different than most roof jobs because the roof was a derby gum roof, something I had never dealt with before. Derby gum is a material that comes in large rolls like felt paper. It's rolled onto the roof like felt, but instead of being nailed down, the rolls are melted onto the roof with fire torches. There was a group of men especially trained to handle the derby gum and apply it to the roof.

After my dreadful day of sweat and labor removing the old roof, this crew would come in like rescuers saving the day from destruction and fire up their torches and go to work. When I saw how cool this job was, I knew I had to be a part of that crew, but I also knew my dad would let me have no part of it. Every day while I was in my pile of torn up roof, loading it down the chute into the truck below, I'd spend a large amount of time watching the derby gum crew, taking in their every move and soaking up their techniques in my mind.

One day when it was time for everyone to go down for lunch, I stayed behind. I grabbed one of the torches and some old pieces of derby gum and practiced burning it on to some old pieces of roof. I started doing this every day. When the crew would return and ask what I was doing with the equipment in my hand, I'd just lie and say I was moving it to clean the mess around it. No one really noticed what I was doing except one of the guys in the crew. He came up the ladder one day and caught me using the torches. Without a word he came over to me and said, "You'd do a much better job if you held the torch this way." From that day on he'd teach me different techniques for using the torch. Each day he'd make sure I had big enough pieces to practice with when everyone went down for lunch. We agreed that my dad couldn't find out about this because I knew he'd blow a gasket if he saw me messing with the torches, not because he's mean, but because he was responsible for getting me home safely.

One particularly hot day I remember it was time for lunch. I walked over to the other side of the roof away from the ladder as I did every day. I counted the overly exhausted bodies going down the ladder one by one. They all filed down like robots on command. When I thought the coast was clear, I grabbed one of the torches and fired it up. The crew had started a roll and never finished rolling it out so I thought this would be my chance to try what I had been practicing for so many days. I started burning the rolls, and to my surprise they came out perfect. Because of the constant practicing my technique was great.

Just as I started to roll my last roll, I noticed a shadow over my shoulder. When I turned around I saw a man standing there looking directly at me like a navy captain about to chew me to pieces. "What the hell are you doing, boy?" my father roared out. I opened my mouth and the only thing that came out was "I...I...I...!" I knew this was it. Nobody did a job on his roof unless he gave the orders.

He approached me and grabbed the spatula and torch from my hand and knelt down beside me. I stood up to take my verbal lashing like a man, but to my surprise my father said, "Kneel your ass down here, boy, and let me show you something!" Without hesitation I knelt down on that roof so fast you never would have known I was standing. I wasn't in for the thrashing I expected. The master was going to teach me and I was ready.

My dad showed me a better technique for seaming the rolls after laying them. Then he looked down the roll I'd already laid and said, "You lay 'em out pretty good." He gave the torch back to me and I started seaming as he'd showed me. As I did that roll I felt him watching over me like a hawk. When I turned to say something to him, he'd gone down the ladder without a word. I didn't mind because at that moment I realized that all my practice had paid off. I finally did something on that roof that made a difference and you couldn't have told me I wasn't great.

Because I practiced it at every moment, I learned that skill and became a member of the derby gum crew, which meant no more labor work for me. My discipline and diligence put me where I wanted to be on that job. Now in my life, I continue to practice in order to be successful.

One last thing about my promotion to derby gum crew: I was still hired help as far as my dad was concerned. I never got a raise.

Have Something to Wake Up For:
God, Family, & Children

Cutting the Cord

Nathaniel Bronner was one of the original founders of Bronner Brothers, maker of African-American hair care products, and I was a good friend of his nephew.

In graduate school, I began attending a church pastored by one of Bronner's sons. Every Sunday the wise and stately looking Mr. Bronner would be standing outside of the chapel after service. My friend and I would go up to him and he'd ask us how we were doing and how my studies were coming. Before we departed, he'd always drop a gigantic nugget of wisdom on us. One particular Sunday he asked me what I wanted to do in life and I went on talking about all the things my doctoral degree would allow me to do.

"By law, I only owe you high school. "
– Willie Mackie Sr.

He listened intently. Then he answered back by telling me that the greatest accomplishment in his life was his family. He talked about his wife and five sons with fervor and ended the conversation by saying, "The greatest tragedy in life is public success and private failure." That message has never left the front of my consciousness as I pursue my dreams.

Like Mr. Bronner, my dad built a business and reared three sons and three daughters. He put all of his money into making sure we had everything we needed to be happy, healthy, and successful. It wasn't until I was older and a father myself that I could fully start to appreciate the sacrifices he made for his children.

As a kid I didn't understand why my dad left home before we awoke in the morning, or why he returned dirty and filthy after dark. I only knew that the entire atmosphere of the house shifted according to whatever mood he was in when he was home. Some nights, after a few beers, he might be talkative. Other nights he'd come home quite stoic and tense, in which case everyone scattered like rats to their respective holes.

My father worked hard and many days I could see the stress marks and strains on his sun-darkened face. Maybe it was the open red flesh on his hand from the splashing of hot asphalt, or the red irritation around his neck from working with fiberglass in hot humid weather — whatever bothered him, he endured it for the sake of his family.

After working during the weekends and summers on the roof, I gradually began to understand some of the sociological issues that plagued many workers at the warehouse. Many, including my dad, abused alcohol extensively. Working through sweat, moans, and groans, while either nailing, lifting, throwing, bending, or standing, places undue stress and strain on the body and the mind. Wiping sweat from your brow with your dirty hands causes red irritated eyes even a bottle of Visine can't help. After a couple of days of enduring the same routine of waking up every morning with an aching stiff back or tender worn hands, all I wanted to do after work was escape this reality as well.

Being too young to drink gave me an interesting perspective relative to the hardened laborers. They needed alcohol after work just to ease the pain and reduce the stress. The alcohol was like a reward worth working toward, especially during the summer months and especially on Fridays. Every Friday at paycheck time was like a holiday. All the men would gather waiting for Santa Claus, my father with the checks. It was an education for me to see the happiness and glee on the filthy dirty worn faces of these men. Through the pain, weariness, and fatigue, smiles and laughter filled the air, as the men told lies and made up stories about what they were going to do that night, usually with women.

One Friday, after everyone had been paid and all that was left in the beer cooler was ice and water, I approached my dad. He was sitting in the quaint dingy office smoking an unfiltered Camel cigarette and drinking an ice-cold Budweiser. He asked me how I was doing and I said okay. He continued looking over the sheets of paper before him while I just stared on. At that moment, I asked my dad to buy me a car; he had bought my older sister and brother cars, and I wanted to know when he was going to give me mine. Hell, I thought he owed me one.

It was the summer before my senior year in high school and I told him that it would be great to go back to school with a new car. He just looked up and said, "What the hell did you just say?"

I told him again that I wanted a car, and then laid my case out on the table. I mentioned that I was an A student, never caused any problems for him or my mother, and that I felt I deserved a car from him. I told him that since I was going to get a scholarship to college he wouldn't have to pay tuition for me, and he could put that money toward buying me a car. Simple as that!

"You finished?" he asked, looking at me with a fierceness that seared into my chest like an infrared laser. I responded, "Yes," and he stood up and now began to talk. With the long cigarette bouncing on his lip as if glued, he went into one of those "end of the world" tirades about how hard he works and how every morning he gets up whether sunshine or rain and goes to work to make sure that the family can eat and have clothes on our back. He talked about growing up without anything and how through sweat, tears, and hard work he provides for his family. He looked in my eyes and made the point clear that he didn't owe me anything. "By law, I only owe you high school," he said.

Then he continued. "Everything you do is for you and your future family … just hope that one day you will be able to provide for your wife and children the way I've provided for you." He concluded his speech by telling me to get the hell out of his office, which I hurriedly did.

I went outside and got into my old Black 1974 Mercury Marquis that could seat an entire basketball team and headed home. However, as I drove I just continued to process his words in my head: "I don't owe you anything... Everything you do is for you and your future family one day…"

I couldn't shake his words then, and I still can't shake them some 20 years later. His statements were profound because it became clear to me that if there wasn't a law requiring parents to care for their children until age 18 or some age of consent, then he might not have given me that much. My father made it very clear that whatever I wanted and was going to get in this world, I had to go get it myself. From that day forward, I never remember asking my father for anything again. I started cutting more lawns, washing more cars, and saving every penny I earned. If he had that attitude toward buying me a car, then I felt I had to be prepared for the day when he really cut the umbilical cord.

At the end of the summer, for the first time, I went shopping for school clothes and purchased them with my own money. I wanted to show my father I didn't need him to give me anything. The only thing I asked for was the minimum, food and shelter. Everything else I tried to earn for myself.

On June 1, 1985, I graduated from high school and six days later my parents delivered me to Atlanta, Georgia to start a summer science program at Morehouse College. I'll never forget the conversation my father and I had while unloading my bags in Atlanta. It was the usual father-to-son type talk where the father explains his expectations to the son. He told me to do my best and explained that he didn't attend college but knew I could handle everything placed before me. He looked around at the other guys and their "educated" parents and told me to remember that they put their pants on one leg at a time just like I did and that hard work will never let me down. In the end, he wanted me to know that I could always come home. He said, "Don't ever think that you are too grown up or educated to come back home. Home will always be there for you."

I had waited for this moment a long time, ever since my father eloquently explained he owed me nothing. After a year, I finally understood what he meant and actually agreed with him, so it was time to close the loop on that conversation.

As he and I walked to the car I just told him that from this day forward I would forever only be a "visitor" at his house. It was my time to really start building a way for myself and my future.

I never called home to ask for money while I was away at school. I took a lot of odd jobs and made a lot of hustles, cutting hair and ironing clothes. Accepting complete and utter responsibility for myself and my future wasn't easy, but I'm a better man for it today, and my family is more financially secure because of it.

Success Starts with Your Family and Those Closest to You

As I continue to grow and develop with children of my own, I admire my dad's strength and determination. When I come home every day and my son runs or stumbles to me I admire my father even more. He had seven mouths to feed and every day he had to wake up and go kill or we'd go hungry.

Recently my father and I were sitting in my backyard sipping some cold beers and exchanging pleasantries and laughter. He looked at my house and said, "Son, I'm proud of you." I responded with a smile and a nod. My son came out of the door and sat in my lap and my father just smiled. He told me he remembered when I was that young. "I didn't know how I was going to do it but every day I got up and went at it," he said. "Now you know exactly how I felt. Now you have a reason to wake up every day and go get it."

Pointing to his grandson he continued, "He doesn't understand 'no food,' or 'I'm tired,' or 'Daddy doesn't have any money.' Your family and your children are the only reason you live. When you forget that or ignore it, you're dead. You should just go dig a hole and get in the ground because you're dead."

These words hit me like a ton of bricks every time I ponder them. My family is my total responsibility now. Everything I do, I do for them. They're the best motivation for getting up and going to work I could possibly have. In fact, my father challenges me now to have more children so that I'll always have a reason to work. When I tell him to hold his horses, he often screams, "Stretch yourself boy! Stretch yourself!"

My dad was definitely the provider in my family. We never wanted for anything of substance like food, clothes, water, and shelter. He made sure his home was taken care of, and that provider attitude is a function of his generation. If there was anything we lacked as children, it was attention and affection.

When my father got home in the evening, he usually had three things on his mind: a bath, dinner, and bed. He wasn't the most talkative or affectionate person during the week. I probably received more face time with him than any of my other siblings because we watched football all day Sunday together and then again on Monday night. For my sisters and my brothers, who were not really into sports, at least not football, their interaction with Daddy was very limited. Like many other men of his generation, my father saw providing for the family as the sole responsibility of the man. Everything else belonged to the woman.

When I graduated from high school, I really hungered to hear my father say he was proud of me. After all, I was graduating number six in a class of nearly 300 people. On graduation day, my father was late getting home and I barely arrived to the graduation on time, which was very necessary because I was sitting on the stage as an honor graduate. We, the graduates, had all been warned that we'd have to sit in the back if we were late. As soon as we arrived at the Jeff Municipal Auditorium in New Orleans, I sprang from the car and ran to make sure I had my place in line. I made it by the skin on my back.

We lined up and the processional began. As we marched into the auditorium, I saw my entire family pressed firmly against the glass door attempting to catch a glimpse of me. I waved and they waved back, but my heart sank to my feet. How could they be late for my graduation? Eventually they were allowed to enter at the end of the procession and watched as I received my high school diploma.

After the ceremony, the graduates exited the building into a sea of people chanting, cheering, and calling out names. I looked and waited to hear my name; eventually I did and I saw my entire family and ran over to them. My mother kissed me, my father shook my hand, and uneventfully we departed. On the way home, everyone in the car seemed upset and perturbed about something or other. We weren't going out to eat or celebrate. We just went home.

Crushed, I changed my clothes and headed out to pick up my girl-friend. I couldn't shake the fact that a big deal had not been made over my graduation, especially after I had done so well in school. The next day I couldn't take it anymore. I meandered around the warehouse all day until my father arrived. I waited until everyone had left, and again he was in his dingy little office going through notes and papers when I entered. He just looked up at me and said, "Whacha say?" I said, "Nothing" and just stood there. He said, "Boy, whacha want, just standing there like you stupid or crazy?"

By this time, tears had begun to swell up in my eyes. I stared at him and finally asked, "Dad, are you proud of me?" "What?" he said. "Are you proud of me?" "What do you mean?"

"I graduated yesterday from school and I want to know if you are proud of me." He said, "What is this about? Do you want a car? Because you know if I had a million dollars I'd give it to you. If I could afford to buy you a car I'd get you ten."

"But, are you proud of me?" I asked again. He responded, "Boy, what in the hell do you want from me?" "Just tell me you're proud of me!" I said. *"Fine. I'm proud of you."*

I turned and walked out of the office with tears rolling down my chin. When I got home, my mother was waiting and it was obvious my father had phoned her. She lit into me before I could get into the door. She was enraged that I would approach my father with such a question considering all he had done for my family and myself. We never were hungry or cold, she reminded me. It became clear my mother didn't understand a child's need for affection from his father. I didn't mean to question his manhood; I just needed to know that he was proud of me. No gift or money was necessary; I only wanted to hear the words from his mouth!

I realized then that material possessions weren't enough to create and support a family relationship. Being a good parent means providing more than just food, clothing, and shelter. You have to provide for the emotional needs of your children as well. To this day, I am eternally grateful to my father for the provisions he made possible for us, but I still yearn for him — the man — and to know that he loves me as his son and is proud of me as a man.

As I travel to juvenile detention centers and jails, I realize that many of the men there still suffer from the pain of having a physically or spiritually absent father. Many young men are walking around with the anger they received from their dad whether he was present or not.

One time when I was speaking in a prison facility I made the statement that our fathers gave all of us something. Suddenly this muscular huge young man jumped up — his chest was big enough for him to wear a bra — and shouted at me, "You don't know what you're talking about. My father never gave me anything. I never even knew my father!" I looked at him, hiding my fear as my heart pounded beneath my shirt and said, "Your father gave you something and I can prove it to you!" "Prove it," he said. I looked at the security officer to make sure he had my back and then said, "I'll prove it... If nothing else, he gave you that anger in your heart. Now you have to learn to deal with it." The young man sat down defeated and the rest of the group sat up appearing more interested in what I had to say.

All of us to some degree have some anger in our hearts for something our mothers or fathers did or didn't do. Like the young man in prison, we have to learn to deal with this disappointment before it overtakes and defeats us. Many of us are walking around in personal prisons, but instead of bars, we're locked up by feelings and emotions.

I'm convinced my father was the best father and family man he knew how to be. He was definitely better than his father, just as your father was better than his father. Our goal is to be much better than our fathers and mothers and bring more completion to the parental figure. No one is perfect. I know I will make mistakes with my children, but I'll attempt to avoid the mistakes my father made with me. I will provide and show affection, and moreover, I will be physically there for my children when they need me.

My father may have provided for us physically, but he wasn't physically there. His absence always bothered me. However, I'll never forget the day I learned why he was never there and it didn't have anything to do with not caring or loving.

On May 31, 1994, my mother passed away and the next day, June 1, 1994, my younger brother and sister participated in their ninth grade promotional exercise from middle school. Less than 12 hours after our mother passed away, the entire family attended the promotional exercise where I was the speaker. After giving a very emotional speech and witnessing my brother and sister graduate from the ninth grade, I joined the entire family outside of the auditorium. To my surprise, my father was standing there dressed in a suit. He had attended the entire event. He told me that my words were quite appropriate and that he was very proud of me, and in turn, I told him I was happy to see him there. He answered rather angrily, "What in the hell do you mean?" I said, "Well, you usually don't come to these type of events and it means a lot to see you here!" His response was very profound. "I had to be here because your mother could not be!" he said.

Whew! 27 years of my life had been explained in that little exchange. It was never that my father didn't care or wasn't interested in my achievements. He just didn't see it as his role to acknowledge them. It was my mother's responsibility to see to those things.

Two years later, when I received my doctoral degree from Georgia Tech, my father was there front and center. When I came off the stage as Dr. Mackie for the first time, I approached him and told him, "This is for you!" For the second time in my life, I saw him cry, with the first time being at my mother's funeral. I realize I couldn't have achieved anything if he hadn't committed to his family, even if it was in his own special way, even if I thought and wished it could have been more. In all of his efforts, without a manual or a guide, he taught me that everything I do is for my future family. He often refers to his great-great grand children not yet born and how he wants them to know that he lived!

My father has taught me a lot about family by the things he did for us, but he taught me even more by the things he didn't do. It's my responsibility to take these lessons and apply them to being an even better parent for my children.

Five Gifts to Give Your Children

Many of the problems and challenges we encounter in today's society can be contributed to the breakdown of the family, especially the extended family. There is an African proverb that says it takes a village to raise a child. I agree with that statement 100 percent.

We have to bring back the concept of the extended family in order to save our children. It's easier to rear and develop children of value, character, and purpose when the community has common goals and interests. As parents, especially fathers, there are five things we should strive to give our children and incorporate into our own lives on a daily basis.

1 The Gift of Love (Self-Assurance and Acceptance)

Love must be something that manifests in our actions every day — in the way we respond to our family and ourselves.

When children know that they're truly loved they're personally protected from many of society's ills. When they lack love, or don't realize they're loved, it creates an emptiness or yearning they will try to fill or satisfy artificially, through drugs, sex, alcohol, and violence.

The word "love" is thrown around so haphazardly now that many people only have a superficial experience with unconditional love, which is supposed to emanate from parents. By unconditional love I mean the love that shines from a mother's eyes toward her newborn. Society's conception of love has been tainted by microwaved 30-second presentations of soap opera love, the spiritually-challenged vile narcissistic love of pop culture, and the trust fund, money-clothes-and gifts-love of broken homes and families. Many individuals only see love and caring through "quid pro quo" eyes, such that, if someone loves them it's only because they expect something in return.

The type of love described above destroys people and families from the inside out. People today are being eaten up by a lack of self-assurance and acceptance. They're yearning to be accepted by anybody and anything because they haven't received the love they need to make them whole. So young men join gangs and call them their families, young ladies get involved with older men too soon, and adults jump from relationship to relationship all in the search for the unconditional love and acceptance they're supposed to get from their parents.

We have to give love in the form of time, energy, and effort. Our families have to know that all of our efforts are for the sole purpose of nurturing, supporting, and reproducing the family for generations to come. This love must be physical, vocal, and spiritual. Show it, say it, and definitely think it! Love begins with the unselfish intention to give all of yourself to others.

2 The Gift of Intimacy (Affection and Touch)

We must touch each other and know that it's okay to show affection for each other. Families and especially children must know intimacy from the home. Don't be afraid to hug, say "I miss you" and "I love you," call just because, or send flowers, cards, and other gifts on any day, not just sanctioned national holidays.

My father isn't a very affectionate person; it's just not coded in his DNA. Most of our interaction took place when we were at work, and our conversations never went beyond sports, roofing, and the lessons of life. We didn't hug. As he has grown older and experienced the cycle called life — burying brothers, sisters, father, mother, and a wife — I believe he's finally begun to understand that it's okay to show affection and express your feelings to loved ones because tomorrow is never promised.

If you love someone, free yourself. Share the gift and tell them today. We're masters of the spoken word and slaves to those that are left unspoken. We're too often afraid of the vulnerability we create in ourselves when we verbally express our emotions and feelings. Sure we're vulnerable, but it's worth being vulnerable to the ones who need to know that we love them.

I've tried to be a more affectionate man than my father. I hug all of my friends every chance I get, and try to feel the pulse of their heartbeats so I know that they're alive. I know some people don't come from touchy-feely homes or backgrounds, but families need to be touchy and feely. Children should receive affection at home so it doesn't seem foreign to them in public. Many young ladies seek approval and intimacy from strangers because they don't receive it at home. If more young women received hugs from their dads, the type of hugs that say "I love you" and "I'm here for you," they wouldn't be as impressed or duped by the insincere words of young Cassanovas. The young ladies would already know that intimacy and love can and do exist without sex.

3 The Gift of Discipline (Self-Responsibility and Assertion)

The best way to give your family and everyone around you discipline is to be a paragon of discipline yourself. A good example is always better than a lecture. Benjamin Franklin captured it perfectly when he said, "Well done is always better than well said."

Many people, including parents, disturbingly subscribe to the adage, "Do as I say and not as I do," thus creating inconsistent and confusing models and choices for those around them. Our families need consistency, especially from mothers and fathers, their top leaders.

Consistency derives from discipline. We all must work to discipline our lives, not to be mechanical, but to be true to ourselves and our words. When we become disciplined studiers, worshippers, employees, husbands, wives, friends, and mentors, people know what to expect from us. Most importantly, they know what not to expect from us. I've often said that the best way to maintain a friendship is by knowing what not to expect from a friend. But we don't have that luxury with our families; they must know that we will be there, that we are accountable — in essence, that we have self-responsibility.

Being responsible helps to develop a strong self-esteem that gives us the power to assert ourselves in powerful caring ways. Discipline breeds confidence because you know, given enough time and the right tools, you can accomplish anything within your grasp. Being disciplined means you're not intimidated by any individual or situation.

Our family and children deserve the right to assert themselves in this world. Give and show them discipline by being a shining example. Dr. Dennis Kimbro, in his bestseller *What Makes the Great Great,* reminds us that "the individual who masters himself or herself through self-discipline can never be mastered by others!"* We must master ourselves first! Then we can be good parents, mentors, and examples for others to follow.

4 The Gift of Character (Personal Integrity and Value)

Character has been defined as what you do when no one else is watching. It emanates from within, but determines a lot of what happens to us in this world. Character can't be purchased, borrowed, or stolen; it has to be earned.

If there's one quality lacking in society now it's character. Many individuals lack values today because again we have learned to compromise our character and rationalize our values to satisfy popular opinions. Society today honors the virtue of wealth rather than the wealth of virtue. We've allowed values and character to be defined by those who are most interested in creating justifications for their actions and defending their positions with half-truths. A rich man can't do any wrong these days. As a matter of fact, whenever their actions or characters are challenged, rich people are usually able to shield themselves behind the fact that they're rich and famous. The marketing of celebrity and fame has created a cult that challenges our values and integrity at their cores. Our children are confused by the hypocrisy, inconsistency, and lack of discipline rampant in all facets of life.

---

* Dennis P. Kimbro. *What Makes the Great Great.* New York: Bantam Dell Publishing Group, 1998. p. 29.

*"Stability in a man's character translates to
normality in his children."*
— Edwin Cole*

Personal integrity and character are the most important traits in each of us and especially within our families. You must have principles to stand on and your family must know this. The world can collapse, but your family must know where you stand. Take a stand on principle and that which you know to be right. A dead fish can go with the flow but it takes a mighty strong one to swim against the current. Don't give into society's current just to go with the flow. Character, values, and integrity are gained and learned when you decide to go against the current, especially when you know that it's flowing in the wrong direction. Your strength will permeate throughout your family, community, and workplace.

Our values keep us centered in a world gone mad. They collectively act as a scale to keep us feeling leveled. When we're off center or operating against our values we know it, feel it, and are stressed by it. The mind was created in truth and when it processes anything else besides the truth, we experience great pain and have to expend greater amounts of energy and effort to get by every day. Follow your values and life will be simpler, better, and less stressful.

---

* Edwin Cole. *Communication, Sex & Money.* Tulsa: Honor Books, 1987. p. 41.

5 The Gift of Purpose (Mission and Direction)

> *"A man's true delight is to do the things he was made for."*
>
> — Marcus Aurelius

I'm a special individual and there's no one else in the world like me. I have talents and abilities to direct and guide my destiny and create my future. The only person who can stop me is me.

To accomplish all of my dreams, I have to get up every day and start working toward my goals. This is what my father taught me through his actions and statements. We must work to give direction to everyone in the family structure and community. Many individuals today are walking around aimlessly as members of the walking, breathing, living dead of America. Our purpose comes from within, initiated and ignited by exposure and experiences. I think the saddest thing in the world is when a person is born and dies in the same place. In a free society, we should exploit the ability to see the world and visit the corners of the universe — physically through travel or mentally through books, libraries, and museums.

Every day, we must attempt to answer the existential questions of "Who am I?" and "Why am I here?" Why are you here? I know I'm here on this earth to serve humankind. And when I serve humankind, I know I'm giving others the ability to follow their dreams and serve humankind also in their own special way.

Use every waking second to find out and pursue your purpose on this earth. Don't settle for just anything that comes your way. You live in a free society, which means you have everything within you to be free, happy, and successful. But your purpose will only be revealed through work and effort. In the end, if you never discover your life's calling or actually touch a life while you're here, you'll have no one to blame but yourself. In essence, the poet summed it up beautifully when he or she said:

> I have only a minute,
> Only sixty seconds in it.
> Forced upon me, can't refuse it,
> Didn't seek it, didn't choose it.
> But it's up to me to use it,
> I must suffer if I lose it,
> Give account if I abuse it.
> Just a tiny little minute,
> But eternity is in it.

You can't expect your children to have a sense of purpose unless you discover your purpose first. Find your goals, create a mission and plan for fulfilling that mission, stick to it, and make it happen. There's always time to raise a family and have children later. Focus on finding your own purpose of life first, then you'll be a true expert when it comes to helping your children find theirs.

WILLIE'S VIEW

The first summer I decided not to work for my dad was hell. I got a job at a local restaurant instead of on the roof with him. The way he acted toward that move was unbearable. You would've thought that I'd asked someone else instead of him to fix the roof on my house.

The rift between my dad and me was not totally my fault. It happened one awfully hot day after working overtime on the roof. When I got back to the warehouse that day, I was tired of the position I was in on the job we were doing, so I made a suggestion to my dad to put me somewhere else. We exchanged a few words and somehow the words "This is my company and I say how things go around here and if you don't like it you can get the hell out," came out of my dad's mouth.

When I looked around, all the men were standing at attention like toy soldiers, in utter disbelief that my father and I were even having this conversation. I turned and looked at my dad and realized how my pride had just been crushed to the point of no recovery. So I did what any hot headed, stubborn Mackie man would do. I walked out. I jumped in the car and went home in a fury. When I got home I started to explain everything that happened to my mother. She got it all. She knew I was mad because I had never spoken so hard about my father in front of her before.

That was it. I was off the roof. In the fall I began working at the restaurant as a dishwasher. My dad was still sore about my quitting, so now there were some new rules. I couldn't use the car to go to work because I got off too late and it was an inconvenience to the whole family.

At the restaurant, some of the guys there formed a group called the Back Hall Gang. We called it that because we'd meet in the back hall of the restaurant to take our breaks and discuss any problems we were having. Our official drink was Fanta root beer.

One evening while discussing the car issue, we decided it was time for us each to get a car of our own. I went home and told my mom about my plans to get a car. I figured this wouldn't be too big a problem for me because when I first started working for my dad he told me that if I did well in school and worked during the summer he'd help me get a car. The only thing that could get in the way was my dad's changed attitude to my new place of work. I made the decision to use my mom as the go-between, but that was no good. She just said I had to take it up with him.

I finally got up the nerve to talk to my dad about the car. I told him that I wanted a car but I'd need his help to get it. He just looked at me like I asked him for the secret code to a bank vault and said, "Boy, I ain't getting you no car, that's out!" I reminded him of the promise about the car he made to me when I first started working with him, but he still balked at the idea. I felt myself getting angry, but I kept it down rather than face my dad's wrath.

I knew I had to do something because everyone in the Back Hall Gang had already secured financing promises on their cars, so I brought it up again later with him. I calmly said, "I'll pay the notes on the car, I just need your help with the down payment. And besides, you promised me this."

Those might have been the wrong words to use. As soon as I finished his ears grew to a point, fangs hung from his mouth, and his head started spinning around on top of his neck. He said, "Let me tell you one thing, I did my part in helping you live and I don't owe you a damn thing. If you want a car go get one!"

I turned toward the house and walked away. As I approached the door I heard my dad call me to come back to him. He never looked at me much, but he said, "If you could save $500 I'll help you get a car. But you have to pay for it." By this time my mom had come into the yard and heard the conversation. "Don't tell that boy that if you don't mean it," she told him. He said, "I know I promised you that and I'll keep my word. Now get the hell away from me."

So now I had a goal. I had to come up with this money. I worked every hour I could to get it, and then it happened, I finally got my $500. I called my job and told them that I'd work the night shift that Saturday because I had to go get my car.

I must have called my dad's warehouse about 100 times looking for him, all to no avail. I sat down on the front porch with my money in my pocket waiting for him to get home. As the evening came I realized that my dad was not going to show up so I asked my mom to take me to work. Normally I'd take the family car, but at this moment I was too stubborn to do that. Out of the corner of my eye I noticed my mom looking at me that whole 13-mile drive. I was very let down.

When I got home that night, my folks were still up. I walked in, said my hellos and went to my room. My dad came in and told me that he'd gotten caught up on a job and couldn't get away. He said we'd get the car next Saturday. I just looked at him like he was transparent. I didn't want to get myself all worked up again for another fall. This was awful because this was something I couldn't do on my own and I knew I needed him, but was next to certain that he wouldn't pull through.

I told myself I wouldn't get worked up, but I did anyway. I couldn't help it. Every day I worked and went home to wait for Saturday. Everyone in the Back Hall Gang got his car and starting on Sunday they'd been asking me questions about mine. When Saturday did come, it found me in my familiar place on the front porch waiting for my dad. I counted 50 phone calls I made to the warehouse to remind him of our date, but he was never there.

Later that afternoon he drove into the driveway. He walked to where I was sitting on the porch and asked if I had all that money with me. I told him yes and he said, "Let's go." On the way to the car lot he reminded me that I had to pay for the car, and the moment I missed a payment he'd take it away from me.

I got my car that afternoon and went straight to work to show it off. It wasn't much of a car, but to me it was the greatest thing I'd ever seen. I worked every shift to make sure I could afford the note.

One day while washing my G-ride, my dad came over to me. "You know, that Saturday you were waitin' for me, I wasn't really caught up on a job," he said. "I just wanted to make sure that you were sure that this was somethin' you could do, you weren't just gonna jump and do it because everyone else was. I never wasn't gonna help you. I made a promise to you, and I'd be nothin' if I broke my word. I see you enjoyin' this little car. Just keep it up, maintain it, and it'll be alright." Then he just walked away. I didn't have a chance for a rebuttal or to even start up another argument. I didn't even want to.

My dad showed me two things that day. Anything worth having is worth waiting for, and a man is nothing without his word.

There's a Time for Work & a Time to Play: Don't Mix the Two

Flying Cookies

The summer months in New Orleans were hot, humid, and filled with fun, even though we spent most of the time outside sweating profusely. Since my father and uncle owned their own company, all of the nephews would work their summers at the company in some capacity. Four first cousins — my brother Willie and I, and two of my uncles' two sons — worked at the warehouse every summer.

As all of us got older, our responsibilities and duties increased accordingly. Eventually, we graduated from the warehouse to the roof during the summers, working as laborers. A laborer had to perform the most humiliating, dirty tasks, devoid of any mental stimulation. A laborer's job was to tear up the old rotten roof, place the debris into wheelbarrows and roll the wheelbarrows across the roof to the orange trash chute where the dumped debris traveled down to the back of a dump truck. Doing this smoothly is harder than it sounds. Packed with that much ripped off roof, the heavy wheelbarrow would wobble, and you'd have to focus your entire attention on maintaining the sucker upright, otherwise it would tip over and you'd have to re-shovel everything back in, breaking your back twice and earning a cold hard stare from my father, the ever-watchful taskmaster.

Working as a laborer was a monotonous back–straining task, but it had its moments. Every day it seemed that something amusing was bound to happen. The question was never if but when one of us would do something so boneheaded that it would send my dad into a mini-tirade or uncontrollable conniptions. Using history as an indicator, we all knew the odds were that my cousin Lawrence from Baton Rouge would be the one to set my father off. It never failed that he would be the one to push the envelope and trample over the prescribed way of doing things.

One summer day we were ripping up a flat roof as usual. It was the longest roof I had seen in my life. There was gravel everywhere and black tar as far as the eye could see, and we all knew it would be a long day. My cousin Lawrence had been complaining that he was hungry the entire morning. While no one was paying attention, he climbed off the roof and went to the truck where he retrieved a box of cookies he had brought with him from home.

Now my father believed in water breaks, because in the Louisiana sun, it was more probable than possible for someone to pass out from the heat or suffer dehydration. But eating while you worked wasn't an option. Food was absolutely forbidden on my father's roof. At lunch he even made sure we didn't eat too heavy because he wanted us ready to work in the hot and humid afternoons.

When we saw my cousin return to the roof with the box, we all won-
dered how he would disguise it, let alone eat the cookies without my
father noticing.

Lawrence, to our surprise, slipped the cookie box down the front of his
pants. As he worked, he would remove one glove, reach down his pants,
retrieve a cookie from the plastic wrapping, and slip it into his mouth,
all before my father could see. This was a bright idea, except Lawrence
had the biggest and most loquacious mouth on the roof. When he was
quiet everyone knew something was wrong.

In order to keep up the act, my cousin had to literally stop, turn his
back from the crew and my father, retrieve a cookie, slip it in his mouth,
and then turn back around again. If this happened once or twice, no
one probably would have noticed, but every time he made it to the
trash chute, he took a quiet little intermission, which was out of the
ordinary for him.

Lawrence made a couple of successful treks across the roof, sneaking
cookies in his mouth and pushing the wobbly wheelbarrow at the same
time. But after catching Lawrence standing at the trash chute with
the wheelbarrow idle, my father started to watch him like a hawk.
He knew something just wasn't right. The routine continued and we
worked moving the trash from the roof to the chute, and after 15 min-

utes, Lawrence went back to eating his cookies. This time he took his little intermission when he returned from the chute back to the work site on the roof.

On one of his passes, my cousin placed two cookies in his mouth and headed to the chute, struggling to keep the wheelbarrow from tipping and chew his cookies at the same time. My father saw Lawrence, and like an All Pro cornerback, he attempted to intercept him before he could make it to the chute. Lawrence, seeing my father out of the corner of his eye, increased his pace but the trash was too heavy, the wheelbarrow too wobbly, and the cookies too full of crumbs. He started to choke. We watched in amazement with tears coming down our face in laughter as my father caught him by the arm and swung him around toward the middle of the roof. Cookie crumbs were flying out of Lawrence's mouth and my father used his free hand to grab the box of cookies from my cousin's pants. Screaming expletives the entire time, my father slung the cookie box off the roof. Customers in the parking lot below must have thought it was raining vanilla wafers.

The rest of the crew couldn't contain themselves as my father chastised Lawrence on his way with his wheelbarrow. Like a drill sergeant blessing out a cadet, my father was in his ear telling him that if he wanted to play — in other words, if he was going to eat cookies and half ass his work — he had to get off the roof. Simply, with the passion and conviction of Denzel Washington in the movie *Training Day*, he told Lawrence and the rest of us that work was work and play was play. We were there to work and anything else besides work wouldn't be tolerated.

We finished that day and eventually finished that job, of course under budget and before the deadline, through sheer hard work and dedication. But not before we learned that cookies could fly.

There Are Prices to Pay for Success — and the First Price to Pay is Hard Work

My father often repeats the old adage that the only place where success comes before work is in the dictionary. For him, there's no substitute for working hard and seeing a job through to completion.

Once you set foot on my father's roof it was all business. There was no such thing as mixing work and play. Every now and then something might happen that would cause the entire crew to burst out in laughter, but it would be my father who would rein everyone back in and get us focused again on the job at hand. He was a master for bringing jobs in under the allotted budgeted time, thus saving on labor and miscellaneous expense costs and maximizing profits. In his world, you work every day and you work hard. After work is the time for beer drinking, clowning, and having all the fun you want with each other, or with him for that matter. He instilled this attitude into his children and carried it to work with him every day. Some might say this work ethic comes from being a self-employed entrepreneur, but I beg to differ. I say he's able to be a self-employed entrepreneur because of this work ethic.

The average worker wants to receive the fruit of his or her labor every Friday or at the end of the month. It's when the check doesn't correspond to the effort or output that we become despondent or unhappy with our work environment. But the boss or the owner is the one who always works longer and harder hours than the regular employees. For that bosses deserve, and usually earn, the bigger paycheck. As author Jawanza Kunjufu stated: "Working hard has always been an admirable goal, slaves did not slow down because they were lazy, but because they were not the beneficiaries of their labor. Employers opt to work longer far more often than employees who require overtime compensation in contrast to the owners who do it for long-term growth." *

In essence, when you work hard it's because you want all the benefit. If you were never trained to work hard or to give your all and to go beyond the call of duty, you'll be satisfied with whatever you receive because you didn't sacrifice anything in the process. When you take pride in your work and effort, you feel as if it's a part of you, that you actually deposited something in the process. You want to see the fruit of such an investment.

Personally, I haven't been able to find anyone who mows my lawn or cleans my house like me. As the owner, I have pride in my home. When I mow the grass, when I sweep my kitchen, when I vacuum the rugs or do the dishes, I put a part of me into it. My father taught us to take pride in our work by putting our all into what we do. There are no places for taking shortcuts. I submit that he is an entrepreneur because he desires the benefit of all his labor. He doesn't know any other way but to put his all into it.

I clearly remember when the New Orleans suburbs were being developed. My father had contracts to perform work on many homes. One Saturday, I accompanied him to work and we worked like dogs for hours. It even began to rain, but we kept at it, working. Naively, I asked my dad why we were still out there and suggested that he could come back Monday. I was ten years old at the most. He turned to me and said, "Boy, this is my business, this is how I put food on the table. If I do not work, you do not eat. We are gonna work until we can't see each other or until the job is finished, whichever comes first."

---

* Jawanza Kunjufu. *Motivating and Preparing Black Youth to Work*. 1ˢᵗ edition. Chicago: African American Images, 1986. p. 34.

We finished the job, we left, and I got the lesson: Have pride in what you do, work to the end, and most importantly own or control something if you want the reward from your labor! This lesson taught me why the manager or owner is the first one in and the last to leave because it's the manager who has responsibility for all that happens. I realized that if I wanted the rewards of the owner or manager I needed to have the traits, habits, and characteristics of an owner or manager. People may be smarter, whiter, blacker, or richer but I have promised myself that no one will out-work me.

Beyond working hard all the time, whenever we start a job or task we should not only finish it, we should focus on doing it right the first time. Double work or having someone come behind you is never good. My father would often ask, "If I got to come behind you and do it, why do I need you?" The work on the roof demonstrated that an assigned task is my responsibility to perform on time within the constraints presented. If there was any doubt that I could do it, then it wouldn't have been given to me. That was the attitude my father had with all of his children and employees. He empowered people, gave them the proper training and tools, and then turned them loose to achieve.

As a kid, my brothers and I had numerous non-negotiable chores. Likes and dislikes were non-existent. We were taught and trained to do what was necessary because that's what my father did. He'd remind us that he didn't get the opportunity to decide whether he liked or disliked going to work every morning, even when he was sick. Why should we get out of performing the chores at home or doing that which was asked of us on the job or roof?

My father takes great pride in his lawn. When he mows the lawn it looks like someone had gotten down on his hands and knees and manicured that thing with a file and nail-clippers. He always expected the same from us. We were required to mow the lawn every week, and when he drove up to our home, my father would give the lawn a fine inspection. The grass was the thick, rich, St. Augustine-type that retained footprints and showed the streaks from the direction in which the lawnmower moved. If the grass was not properly mowed, the streaks told no lie.

One Friday evening, my older brother Willie rushed home from school and haphazardly cut the grass. He was in a hurry because the school dance was that night. I watched as he butchered the yard cutting against the grain, going north, south, east, and west, randomly with no specific order or methodology. The results weren't good. He came in the house, jumped in the shower, and put on his best dress pants and shirt, preparing to go to the dance. Sitting downstairs in the kitchen I heard my dad's truck pull up in the driveway. After a minute or two he rushed into the house looking disheveled and angrily asked if I'd cut the grass. "Nope," I told him, "Willie did it!"

About that time my brother came downstairs and turned the corner into the kitchen looking and smelling completely fresh and clean. My father told him that the yard looked like shit and told him to cut it again. My brother sighed and said, "Okay, I'll cut it tomorrow. I gotta get to a dance at school." My father looked at him and said, "No you are not! You're gonna go cut the grass."

Now angry, Willie turned to go back upstairs and my father asked, "Where are you goin'?" My brother said he was changing clothes so he could go back and mow the lawn. My father said, "No you're not. You're gonna go cut the grass just like you are." He stepped to the door and opened it for Willie. Willie re-cut the grass in the dark wearing his best dress clothes. The following morning my father woke him up early and made him mow it again in the daylight! Wow! I watched in amazement. This was some crazy stuff.

Later that Saturday when my father came home, he called us together. I feared he was going to make Willie cut the grass again, or worse, make both of us cut it. However, he told us that he did what he did for a purpose and the purpose was to teach us that if you do your work right the first time you won't have to do it again. It takes the same amount of time to do it right as it does to do it wrong, he said, so do it right the first time.

· ·

"If anyone will not work, let him not eat."
— II Thessalonians 3:10

· ·

Now I see that my father was on to something that burned deep in his gut. Many people consider work a curse, but it's actually a blessing and possibly each person's salvation. It's easy to work hard at something you love. You must find work that you love and you'd perform for free. I know, I'm repeating myself, I wrote it plenty of times earlier in this book, but if you love what you do, doing it for free won't be necessary. When you love what you do and invest your heart and soul into it, people will pay for your services without you necessarily seeking them out. Others will be so impressed with your work, they'll tell the world — and work, money, wealth, and meaning will arrive at your doorstep. In *What Makes the Great Great,* Dennis Kimbro wrote, "What the age wants are men and women who have the nerve and the grit to work and wait, whether the world applauds or jeers."*

---

* Dennis P. Kimbro. *What Makes the Great Great.* p. 175.

We're living in a time of overindulgence and excess. Many young individuals entering the workforce have never really had to work hard. I was amazed during the 2004 presidential debates between President George W. Bush and challenger Senator John Kerry by a certain comment the President made. Every time he attempted to describe his programs and policy over the last four years, he would end his comments or begin them by stating, "This is hard work!" News organizations reported that he used the phrase "hard work" 11 times during the 90-minute debates. Listening to him gave me the impression that he didn't realize that being the President of the United States and the Free World was going to require real hard work. He actually seemed surprised.

Many of my students return to campus and with amazement explain to me that their jobs expect them to work hard with long hours. Life and especially work are no walks in the park and like President Bush, all of us will eventually realize it. Due to birthright, family, or inheritance, we may be able to escape the challenge of hard work, but those who never have to work never discover the true capacity of who they are and what they're capable of achieving. Work, real work with real effort, heart and soul, meant to serve humankind, has benefits far beyond wealth.

Work is an awesome teacher. It teaches humility, appreciation, patience, compassion, discipline, perseverance, sacrifice, and reward. You really can't appreciate someone's accomplishments until you understand and experience what it took for such an achievement. Working toward a goal develops patience in the impatient if success is accomplished, because achievement doesn't occur overnight or spontaneously. Excellence usually comes from serious repetition preceded by initial failure. You will meet humility on the road to success. The goal is to pick it up and keep it by your side for sustained success and achievement.

Discipline is doing what you have to do when you have to do it and work becomes simple and more rewarding when you're disciplined. Middle Americans and those in the rural parts of this world understand that before the reward there must be labor. You plant before you harvest, sow in tears before you reap joy. A mother goes through hours of hard difficult labor before bringing forth a bundle of joy. A masterpiece isn't a masterpiece until after the artist labored day and night alone, placing paint upon a bare canvas.

Frederick Douglass said that those who want success without work are like those who desire crops without plowing the ground, the ocean without the mighty awful roar of its water, rain without the thunder, the progress without the struggle, and that's just not possible.* Work is not for quitters! When properly pursued and performed it'll definitely teach perseverance. In order to achieve goals or bring the job to closure we must persevere to the end. As soon as the road gets tough, many people jump off of the wagon, but you won't ever be successful in life unless you ride it out until the end.

Graduate school was a difficult challenge for me. The effort required just to compete seemed almost impossible at times. The pain of staying up night after night and working sometimes 100 hours a week to teach a lab, do coursework, and perform research all while studying for qualifying exams at the end of the semester forced me to reach deep within myself. Often I found myself curled in the fetal position on the floor in the middle of the night crying because the work was so tough and lonely. Many times I considered quitting but I had to finish the degree to do what it was I wanted to do. I already had a mathematics

---

* Frederick Douglass. Letter to an abolitionist associate. August 3, 1857. Published in *Organizing For Social Change: A Mandate For Activity In The 1990s.* Edited by K. Bobo, J. Kendall and S. Max. Washington, D.C.: Seven Locks Press, 1991.

degree and an engineering degree. Corporations were offering me jobs with high salaries every semester but I wanted something else. I wanted more. I wanted the doctoral degree. Like being President of the United States, earning this degree would be hard work, but working on the roof, watching my father work 30 years in the most inhumane and challenging conditions, had prepared me for the task.

The next time you see someone you consider successful, ask yourself "Am I willing to do what he did to get there?" If you answer in the affirmative, then start doing things the way they did them. Approach your work and goals with the same tenacity, discipline, and sacrifice your role models employed to achieve their dreams.

Achieving the doctoral degree in mechanical engineering took me 11 years past high school. While others were partying and going to football games and happy hours, I was studying, reading, building, and explaining. Work and achievement definitely teaches sacrifice. There's a price to be paid for success and the first price is work — hard, serious work.

Six Ways to Increase Your Work Output

To pay the price and increase your capacity to perform hard work, commit to do the following each day. Your productivity will increase and you'll see measured results in your life and work.

1 Understand and accept that you control your destiny

Take personal responsibility for your actions, or more importantly, control your actions. Map out your future and work toward it every day.

2 Start where you are with what you have

As the NIKE ads implore: Just Do it! African-American folklore says, "God makes three requests of his children: do the best you can, where you are, with what you have, now." Do your best and push yourself beyond the usual limits. Raise your expectations of yourself and everyone around you.

3 Set goals and outwork yourself each successive day

Compete against yourself. Stop measuring your achievement against others and better yourself every day by stretching your effort to levels you've never experienced.

4 Become a creature of habit

Learn to do a task right and do it correctly all the time. Seek to perfect your efforts and repeat the task the same way every time. Discipline your life and experience your fullest potential.

5 Find an accountability partner

This is someone who'll be honest with you and properly evaluate and gauge your personal improvement or lack thereof. Mentors come in all shapes, sizes, and colors. You can learn from anyone who is willing to share his or her experiences. Respond to those who have high expectations of you.

6 Motivate yourself

Learn and recite the following statement from author Maltbie D. Babcock and make it a daily affirmation:

We are not here to play, to dream to drift,
We have hard work to do, and loads to lift,
Shun not the struggle!
Tis God's gift!
Be Strong.*

---

*Benjamin E. Mays. *Quotable Quotes of Benjamin E. Mays.* New York: Vantage Press, 1983. p. 1.

WILLIE'S VIEW

My dad had a lot of young men working for him. Some of them were in trouble with the law and others just needed cash in their pockets. My job, aside from all the labor, was always to be the token. If the owner's son can do manual labor, why shouldn't they?

On one job I remember, two other guys and I had to get a dump truck full of gravel from the ground to the roof. Our tools consisted of two wheelbarrows, three shovels, and a rope and pulley with a bucket attached.

To make it easier on ourselves, the three of us came up with a plan: I'd bring the gravel half way to the pulley and give it to the second guy, he'd bring it to the guy at the pulley, and then that guy would load it into the bucket and hoist it up to the roof. We did this so we wouldn't tire ourselves out in the hot sun and we planned it so we'd all have an equal load to bear.

This worked out fine at first. The only real problem was that the guy who was handling the rope and bucket, a young kid we called Pickle, was a bit of a clown and ran his mouth off better than he ran the pulley. To make matters worse, he'd constantly go up the ladder to see what was going on and to harass the men on the edge of the roof. The other guy in my crew and I just continued to load the gravel next to the place where Pickle was supposed to send it up. We knew if that gravel didn't get up there and my dad found out about it, all hell would break loose.

Everybody on the job site could see a disaster coming on the horizon because Pickle just wouldn't stay at his station long enough to get the gravel on the roof. We all waited until there wasn't any more gravel to see what my dad would do. I knew it the minute they ran out. I heard my dad screaming from the top of the roof: "Gravel man! Gravel man!" He came to the edge of the roof and screamed again, but there was no answer. By this time, every worker on the roof had stopped working to come look down over the side and see what was going on. My dad made his way down the roof and saw a large pile of gravel, an empty bucket, and no one there to get it on the roof.

"Where in the hell is that boy Pickle?" As I stood at attention I told my dad I didn't know where Pickle was. My wheelbarrow and the other wheelbarrow were full of gravel, so at least the other guy and I could say we'd been working. My dad continued to scream "Gravel man! Gravel man!"

That was when Pickle, the gravel man, happened to come right from the other side of the building. He didn't see my dad at first, but when he finally noticed he tried to run. He'd positioned himself between my dad and the back of a truck and couldn't get away.

I saw my father start toward Pickle, but he stumbled on the gravel and fell over. We all started laughing so hard we couldn't talk. When my dad got back on his feet he had a handful of gravel. He screamed, "I need this damn gravel on the roof!" Then, to the surprise of us all, he threw the handful of gravel at Pickle. He ducked, and when he came up he told my dad "Well, you don't have to throw that gravel at me." This was more than any of us could take. We were in stitches. My dad bent down and got another handful of gravel and threw it at Pickle again.

My dad ordered Pickle to come over to him and like a little puppy obeying his master Pickle went. My dad told him that this was work and not a playground. "If you want to play, stay home!" Pickle said okay, but then went on to protest again about being hit with rocks. My dad moved to get another handful and Pickle went running to the other side of the truck. When my dad climbed back up the ladder, everyone who had stopped working to look down scattered like a gang of mice when you turn the light on. It was back to work.

We laughed about this scene for days, but we all know how my dad felt about work. We made the best of every moment on that roof. We had to. For most of the men there, that's all they knew.

Have Pride in an Honest Day's Work

Po' Boy

One morning at the warehouse all of the men had gathered for their respective crew assignments, while Willie and I stood by and watched. After assigning the men to their respective crews, my dad realized that the crew working on the big Kmart store project was going to be short some workers. This was crucial because the Kmart job was behind schedule and each day we worked over schedule was time that ate into my father's calculated profits.

My dad turned to my brother Willie and I and said he needed us on the roof. We usually spent our days at the warehouse loading trucks, driving the forklifts, and designing sheet metal jobs, but this day we were going to be used for hard labor. When we heard the bad news, we both let out a groan.

Working on a job site required you to endure tough, backbreaking labor in the harshest environments — high temperatures, dense humidity, and hot asphalt tar. On site, our job would be tearing and ripping up the roof and transporting the pieces to the garbage chute. This was intense labor with very few breaks in between.

That morning on the Kmart site was the hottest morning of my young life. Immediately on the roof, sweat began a natural trek from my forehead to the cusp of my dimpled jaw. With flat spade shovels in our hands, we cut and dug into the old worn rotten roof, which was about three inches thick with insulation, asphalt, and gravel. We wrapped our necks with saturated towels, attempting to keep the flying fiberglass from settling in the crevices close to our shoulders. Dust particles and fiberglass clouds engulfed us with every shovel thrust into the deteriorating roof and every bump we hit pushing the wobbly wheelbarrow to the orange dumpster chute. All the while I thought to myself, *there's no way this could be a healthy work environment.* I was sure I was inhaling poisonous particles, but I knew better than to complain about this to my father, who had probably inhaled enough dust in his life to leave his lungs permanently black.

By noon our clothes were filthy and soiled with dust. All the workers climbed from the roof preparing for the usual lunch — an hour marked by mingling and self-deprecating joking that tied our stomachs in knots with laughter. As we gathered around the water cooler customers filed in and out of the Kmart, cars raced around the parking lot, and the conversation turned to the lunch menu.

One of the other workers indicated that there was a deli in the Kmart that sold the famous New Orleans Po' Boy sandwiches. Po' Boys are famous for their excessive meat and condiments stuffed between a soft nine to 12 inch long roll of freshly baked French bread. My father, some of the other workers and I decided to go inside and get a couple of these delicious Po' Boys for our lunch.

As we walked toward the door into Kmart, I suddenly became apprehensive and slowed my pace. Always attentive, my father noticed this change and questioned, "Boy, don't you want to eat?" Looking frustrated and unsure, I answered, "Yes!" He said, "Well come on... we have to eat and get back to work." I didn't move and my father grew anxious and flustered. With an intense tone of voice he asked, "Boy, what is wrong with you?" I told him I didn't want to go into the store because I was dirty and all the other people at the store were not.

He walked up to me until he was right in my face. Sternly he said, "Let me tell you one thing, you are dirty because you are making an honest day's work. I know your mother would never allow you to go anywhere looking as you are now, but you are here working, making a living. Boy, don't you ever feel ashamed of making an honest living. Anyone in this place who doesn't respect that or you can go to hell. You're not stealing or begging and regardless of how you look, you don't have to apologize to anyone or feel bad about it. Now get your ass in here and get some lunch."

I listened intently and made my way into the store with him in tow. We walked into the Kmart and got in line. My father had his hand on my shoulder and I could see the dignity and pride in his eyes. He wasn't only providing for his family, he was providing for 50 families, by giving all of the men on his crew a chance to earn a livelihood. The men respected him for that and definitely for his work ethic.

Dirty or not, my father was always proud of the contributions he was making to my life and the lives of the people around him. After that day, I never again felt a sense of shame for the sweat and dust I earned from a hard day's work. In fact, today I take pride from it.

There is Honor and Dignity in Whatever You Do as Long as You Are Adding to Society and Not Taking Anything Away From It

Having pride in an honest day's work is one of the principal tenets of the America Dream.

In America, you can wake up every day and begin to shape and mold your future. Regardless of your race, sex or gender, you have the ability to make sure that today will be better than yesterday. It is true that some individuals may have institutional advantages over you due to race, gender, or socioeconomic class. They may have an easier route in this world, but you still can get up and take pride in what you're doing, especially if you're doing it without violating anyone's rights or breaking any laws.

My father with all of his eighth grade education is proof that you can shape yourself and your family, and impact families and communities around you as well. Many of his employees respected him for the opportunities he provided them and really didn't know what they'd be doing if he hadn't taught them a trade. He demonstrated to all of us that our work and efforts in society were just as important as any doctor's, lawyer's, or engineer's contributions.

On and off the roof, he taught me to respect all people regardless of what they do as long as they are making an honest, respectable living. Even today, I walk into hotels and marvel at the humility of people who clean the rooms and serve the food. They make it possible for us to do our jobs by providing the opportunity to rest or work in a comfortable and clean place. They go about their tasks without the fanfare or the recognition the concierge or manager receives even though the hotel could not operate efficiently or profitably if they did not perform their jobs honorably. The service staff is as important as any other professional employed at the hotel. At the end of the day, they may not be the cleanest people around, but the labor required by their work probably insures that they are among the most tired. These people should leave every day with their heads held high and their pride and dignity intact for they're earning an honest living.

Consider public servants like policemen and fireman who risk their lives so we can have an orderly and safe society, a society governed by laws rather than mob rule. What would our lives be like if policemen didn't take pride in their work or believe in the mission statement of their profession — "To serve and protect?"

We may have forgotten that firemen place their lives on the line for us every day, but the tragic terrorist events of September 11 brought back the harsh reality of their profession and demonstrated the respect and gratefulness we owe them. It wasn't fame or riches, but their pride in their work that compelled those firemen to rush into those burning buildings. They knew they had a job to do. Every time I see a red fire truck racing somewhere I can't help but to consider the dangers the firemen will be facing shortly and I pray that each of them will return home safely.

Sometimes it seems that society only respects those professions that produce large salaries and great wealth. Doctors, lawyers, and well-heeled businesspeople who drive fine cars and live in large homes receive most of our admiration. Teachers and other public servants are often forgotten while they endure the brunt of keeping society safe, clean, and educated. This is wrong, especially when we consider how many teachers and public servants have impacted our own lives. If anything, they deserve the most respect for serving humankind on small salaries.

If working on the roof didn't teach me to respect the dignity and importance of other people's work, living in Charlotte, North Carolina for a summer, while interning at a major corporation, definitely did. It was the first time I overtly experienced classicism and elitism up close and personal.

Our research facility was divided into four basic categories: service staff, technicians, engineers, and management. How you were treated and respected was dictated by your job description and education. As you can imagine, the service staff and technicians were treated with the least amount of respect, mainly because their education was below or on par with a high school degree.

It was difficult for me to treat the service people or technicians with any less respect than I gave my fellow professionals, simply because anyone in my family could have had those jobs. Instead of looking down on them, I empathized with them and made sure that I acknowledged them in everything I did. I gave them a respectful greeting every morning and told them to have a good evening at the end of every day. I became fast friends with all of the service staff and technicians only because I constantly demonstrated respect to them. They in turn went the extra mile for me on numerous occasions, giving me special preference when there was a backorder for their time.

This experience with classicism taught me a valuable lesson about business: everyone contributes in a successful organization, from the landscaper to the CEO. Everyone, therefore, should be made to feel as if they are part of something special and the organization cherishes their contribution. It was because I treated the staff and service people as human beings as opposed to low-status employees that they were there for me when I needed them. No one is below equal treatment. The best leaders know this and do their best to communicate respect to others through their actions every day.

Giving people their due respect can be challenging. It pushes us to overcome the biases and preconceptions we inherit from our families and communities. Most of all, it requires us to push past our habit of thinking negatively about people who seem different. It forces us to break out of our comfort zones and approach people at the level of their point-of-view.

There was one person at the research facility that summer who people repeatedly warned me about. His name was Bobby and he was a technician with a fondness for southern history, especially Confederate and Civil War history. In fact, Bobby reenacted the Civil War once a month as a Confederate soldier. This did not bother me at all, because as far as I was concerned, the Confederates lost, which meant that Bobby would eventually get killed. And yet he seemed to dodge the Blue coats' bullets every month! When I would walk into the lab and see the Confederate hat on his desk, I'd just let out a big sigh and continue about my business.

From day one, Bobby greeted me and treated me with the utmost respect, and I reciprocated. Eventually, I asked Bobby to lunch and we had a great time, an absolute ball in fact. One Friday we ended up at a local joint called "Aw Shucks," which was a Louisiana Cajun-style restaurant and pub with a patio attached to the rear facing train tracks. On the patio was a big sign that stated "Please Do Not Throw Bottles at the Train." The pub sold long neck beers by the pail, and after a pail or two, I heard the whistle of the locomotive coming from afar. Bobby furiously began to rush down beers. Then suddenly he looked at me and said, "Hurry up the train's comin'." I finished the rest of my beer and pulled some empty bottles closer to me and when the train got there, Bobby and I pummeled it with every bottle we had. We threw bottles, laughed, and slapped high fives as the train passed.

Bobby continued to fight the Civil War once a month and we continued to work together in harmony. I accomplished a lot that summer thanks to his guidance and direction. While I didn't agree and still don't agree with the romanticizing and reliving of the Civil War, I respected Bobby for who he was and what he had to bring to the organization. He reciprocated that respect, and that's all I can ask for from any person. Every day he and I put in an honest day's work together, and the results were amazing.

At the end of the summer, the human resources director told me she had been concerned about placing me in the lab with Bobby, but that everybody was absolutely amazed by how I handled the situation and managed to build a strong relationship with an apparent bigot and redneck. When she asked me how I did it, I just told her what my mother always said to me: that manners and respect will take you places money cannot and will not. I also told her what my father taught me: to respect and have pride in an honest day's work. The way I saw it, the technicians, service staff people, and I were all one and the same. To disrespect any of them would be like disrespecting my father, mother, aunts, ancestors and most importantly myself! Bobby and I may have looked and seemed different on the outside, but we had a lot in common when we both looked past that and grew to respect each other for the quality of work we did in our respective fields.

In hindsight, I realize that my time on the roof had prepared me for the hard work ahead of me, as well as the situations I would encounter later in my career. It taught me to respect what everyone had to bring to the table, even if some of those people turned out to be Civil War re-enacting, pseudo-Confederate soldiers like Bobby. Most importantly, it taught me to invest equal passion and commitment in everything I did, no matter how tedious the work. This attitude has continually attracted attention and paid off throughout my life.

The same summer of my engineer internship I met a gentleman by the name of Don Baker. I was playing basketball in South Park on Archdale Drive in Charlotte one afternoon. He jumped in and we started talking. He was 20 years my senior, but he took an interest in who I was and where I came from. I explained to him that I was a summer intern at a local chemical company and new to the area. We met in the park every evening after that to play ball, and eventually he invited me to his home for dinner with his wife and children.

Don was an entrepreneur who owned a janitorial company and asked me if I wanted to make some additional money for school and I jumped at the offer. Every evening from 6 to 9 PM, Don had crews cleaning office buildings in the area. I eventually joined one of the crews in charge of cleaning the corporate headquarters of a local firm. Don showed me the ropes, teaching me such things as the proper way to place toilet tissue in the dispenser (with the tissue hanging over the roll rather than under), and how to mop a marble floor without leaving streaks or footprints.

After a couple of weeks, Don actually turned the entire building over to his cousin and me, and trusted us to clean the building accordingly. He personally directed me on how to clean the CEO's office, which was a great responsibility because the CEO had many pet peeves in terms of how he wanted his office cleaned every evening. For example, he didn't want to see tracks or steps in his three-inch plush carpet. Instead he wanted to gaze upon a sea of undisturbed gray carpet when he opened his door every morning. For that reason I had to vacuum the office in such a way that when I backed out of the office I had to cover over my last footprints in the carpet. This meant that all the other cleaning had to be completed before I started vacuuming. If something remained undone in the office and I had to return to complete it, I had to vacuum the office all over again. It was a pain sometimes, but I took great pride in this job and the responsibility placed in me.

One evening, I was cleaning while the CEO of the company was still in his office, working continuously and ferociously at his desk. I had already cleaned the halls and the adjoining office and was sitting on the floor in the hall waiting for him to leave. Eventually he noticed me and asked if I was waiting to clean his office and I answered in the affirmative. He beckoned me in and told me to go about my business and just ignore him. I began cleaning, dusting, and dumping the trash with all the zeal and zest we put into our work every night. I noticed him watching me and suddenly he blurted out that he appreciated the care and effort I put into cleaning his office. I responded by saying, "Thank you, sir!"

He asked how old I was and I told him that I was 20. He went on to tell me how important education was and that in the future education would become even more important. He also told me that I should put the same energy, effort, and pride into my education and my future would be bright.

When he finished talking, I informed him that I was a summer engineering intern at the research facility of a national corporation located right there in Charlotte. I explained I was a rising junior in college majoring in math and mechanical engineering. With a surprised look on his face, he asked me what I was doing cleaning offices. I said it was an opportunity to make some additional money for the academic year. The CEO seemed stunned that someone with my education would be cleaning offices, and said, "You definitely take pride in your work, keep it up!"

When he said those words, my mind quickly harkened back to Kmart and my father's lesson about taking pride in an honest day's work. By recognizing me and my efforts, the CEO was also recognizing the fruits of my father's labor, and it made me feel proud to know I was continuing the reputation for hard work that went hand in hand with the Mackie name.

Too many business leaders overlook, neglect, and downright disrespect people who wear uniforms, clean their offices, or serve them their food. They never stop for a moment to consider how impossible it would be to work and profit without such individuals. These hardworking souls don't make strategic decisions or comment on quarterly profits for shareholders, but they are core components of the business's total success. They're truly the silent unsung heroes.

Having pride in your work should be a core value in business as in life. In the age of individualistic mass consumerism and blatant materialism, America has lost this value. People are valued now by how much they earn. Shortstops in baseball make a salary 100 times greater than that of a teacher, and business executives now draw salaries 50-100 percent higher than that of the average employee.

Watch television and you will believe that everyone is rich and that something is wrong with you if you're not. The promise of America is not riches but the opportunity to pursue the dreams and desires of your heart. This promise has been displaced by a desire for the short-term gain and instant gratification. Because we no longer value people for the honest moral work that they do, most people will attempt anything possible to amass wealth, no matter how criminal or baseless. For these actions, they're rewarded, or at the very least, punished just a little. Those few people attempting to be ethical can't help but feel like suckers when they see criminals and thieves succeeding despite breaking the law.

> *"The poor and ignorant will continue to lie and steal as long as the rich and educated continue to show them how."*
> – Unknown

Look to the examples provided by Worldcom, ImClone, and Enron. Millions of people were hurt when their retirement accounts were depleted after these corporations collapsed due to the amoral and unethical behavior of their leadership. At some point, some very smart, well-educated people saw a way to profit without having to work too much or too hard. By taking the easy way out, the unethical way, they in turn short-changed a lifetime of wealth the hardworking people in their companies had saved up. This wasn't just a matter of cheating people out of a few bucks — whole families, futures, and inheritances were destroyed.

We have watched for years as the so-called elite and educated have committed numerous white-collar crimes only to walk away unscathed or with a slight slap on the wrist, while the common man busts his butt every day to do what is right, moral, and upstanding. It's nearly impossible to teach youth to have pride in an honest day's work when their role models and leaders are showing them something entirely different.

I once heard a wise individual say, "The poor and ignorant will continue to lie and steal as long as the rich and educated continue to show them how." At some point, we have to break the mold, think for ourselves, and look for ways as a society to recapture a sense of pride in our work and ourselves, no matter how much we're paid. Children have to see that they too can benefit and learn from hard, backbreaking work. They have to see that while shortcuts may make us wealthy, they rob us of something else, namely dignity and self-respect.

My father through his unorthodox, tough love manner taught me that you feel better about yourself, your work, and your career when you can take pride in the work you perform every day, in the people you work with, and in the institution for which you work. Having a sense of pride in your work may be difficult in today's world, but it's something I believe can be truly achieved and maintained if we only learn how to adopt the right attitude toward what we do.

Three Ways to Develop Pride in Your Work

Each person should focus on developing and maintaining pride in his or her work by seeking these three things:

1 Control: Effectively manage yourself and your responsibilities

As an individual, you can carve out a niche, a specialty which you and you alone control. You can come to understand your job inside and out to the point that you know what it takes to be successful, and how to get the best possible and complete result by effectively managing yourself and your responsibilities. Empower yourself to accomplish a task before it's requested by always ending the day with a list of what needs to be accomplished tomorrow in order to complete your responsibilities. As a kid I learned early on that I could do almost everything I wanted if I did the chores requested of me first. I didn't wait around until I was directed because I already knew what needed to be done. Take control of your little sphere of existence regardless of what others are doing, and take pride in your independence, self-reliance, and discipline.

If you're a trash handler on a construction site, you want to make sure that the presence of trash won't be an obstacle to completing the job. Repairs and building can't occur until the debris has been properly removed and disposed of. This doesn't mean you have to become the construction supervisor and take control of the job, it simply means that you should take control and responsibility for the outcome of your efforts regardless of your place in the managerial chain or how your boss or supervisor responds.

Try to observe and understand how your work fits into the mission of the team. You don't need to be the team leader or have the most visible responsibility to play a vital role in the victory and success of the team. You just have to take control of your responsibilities and make sure you're not the weak link in the food chain. The janitorial staff at schools should know and take pride in the fact that they have played instrumental roles in the lives of all of the students and staff by creating an environment conducive to positive work and excellence! You should likewise celebrate when your team and organization scores a victory.

I often hated working on the roof, especially when I found myself struggling to push the heavy-loaded wheelbarrow of trash to the dump chute. It all seemed worth it, however, when I was able to look at the finished product and know that the occupants of this house could now accomplish their daily tasks and live unencumbered by weather. I took pride in my part and effort. I saw where and how my niche — wheeling trash to the dumpster — fit into the Big Picture of building these people a better roof.

2 Significance: Determine the importance of your work

Working on the roof, I often observed the significance of my duty to the group and company. I saw how my job allowed the company to be profitable, and as a result how it allowed the other men to get their paychecks every week and create opportunities to hire even more employees.

Many people get caught up in titles without realizing that work is the real engine driving the success of a project. It's like the hotel housekeepers: If they don't do their jobs with pride and diligence, I promise you that hotel will fail.

Work pride emanates from the role your effort plays in the outcome of the project. You can't wait for someone else to articulate the significance of your work because if someone can establish that significance, then they're empowered to remove or diminish that significance as well.

Your work has to be significant to you first and foremost. You have to understand that for yourself and operate from that perspective. Seek to understand the direction of the company or organization. How does your task benefit and support the mission and direction? How does your task benefit the group? Could the group achieve its mission without your task being accomplished? If so, then you need to seek another task or group.

3 Recognition: Accept credit for your contribution

When you take pride in your work, others will notice and recognition will come. It may come in the form of increased tips, a raise, a promotion, or a positive comment that seers into your heart.

Don't seek recognition just for the sake of recognition. Seek to do an excellent job that begets recognition. Even the most poorly trained supervisor or manager will eventually recognize work into which someone has poured their heart and soul because the quality of the work will speak for itself.

Sometimes we have to acknowledge ourselves in our own special way. In big groups and organizations, people are sometimes overlooked. That's why it's important to take control of our responsibilities and determine the significance of our work for ourselves. At the end of the day, we have to be able to leave work and arrive again the next day with pride in what we do, regardless of the level or lack of recognition received.

WILLIE'S VIEW

Pride is something that my father wore on his shoulders like a fresh suit. You saw it in his face and you heard it in his conversation. He was proud of his decision to be a roofer and he freely inserted his craft into every conversation he was involved in. Nothing on earth was more important than what he did. I heard him compare his work with lawyers, doctors, and corporations and he hung himself in there with the best of them.

He taught me about pride at a very young age. When I was in my teens my dad decided to build us a new home. I was involved in every aspect of this venture from designing the place to hammering that last nail into the wall. I enjoyed this because it really gave me a sense of self worth. I worked with the plumber, the electrician, and the bricklayer to get this house perfect. Anyone who was involved in the place had to be involved with me. This was great for me. I threw my name around like I was the President of the United States, telling people what to do and how to do it. I got a big head about this job and about me.

I remember one day my dad and I had to pick the light fixtures for the house. We made plans to meet my mother at home and then leave to meet the man at the lighting warehouse. When I got home my dad was already waiting for me. He was sitting in the den with his green Dickeys uniform on and that little checkered cap that he wore all stained with tar. He looked at me and asked if I was ready. I replied "Yes, but aren't you going to change your clothes?" He said "Hell no! What's wrong with what I got on? I got to go back to work after this. I'm not goin' to impress nobody." I knew at that point I'd touched a nerve so I just took it all in. He continued, "These clothes are good enough for me to take care of you, so they should be good enough for you to be seen with me in 'em."

I noticed he was getting upset so I backed off. But in the car he still kept going on about my comment and it sunk in.

I'd become somewhat of an ass. My dad had been wearing the same clothes as long as I could remember and never complained about it. Everywhere I went with him he was in his work clothes, and now I'd questioned him about that same suit of clothes he wore to put food on the table and nicer clothes on my back. I sat there that day and wanted to apologize, but like him, my pride was a huge factor in my life, and it just wouldn't let me do it.

After we selected the lights he brought my mom and me home and headed back out the door. As I watched him leave, I realized that our fight wasn't about the clothes but about the status of what we were becoming that I got caught up in. I may have thought I was the President, but I was really just old Willie Mackie. I really felt bad because my parents never instilled a status-seeking drive in any of us.

Later that day I had to go back to the site where the house was being built to look after everything there. When someone asked me something about the house, I was a little more hesitant to give him or her the gospel according to Willie Mackie Jr. Now I just said I'd call my dad and find out.

137

Don't Fear Evaluation of Your Work: Invite It!

"Excellence is to do a common thing in an uncommon way."

— Booker T. Washington

The Qualifiers

My father has always taken serious pride in the craftsmanship of his work. I remember riding around with him in his truck as he pointed out the roofs he had previously done and the special problems each job presented for him to solve. You could tell from the tone of his voice that a commitment to excellence is a core value of his business mission and work ethic.

He often said, "Service your clients and they'll tell someone else about your business." A client could call during the middle of a hurricane and he'd run out the door to correct an error or repair a leak. Even if the client was wrong, my father tried his best to resolve the issue, because he knew that one unsatisfied client could cost him 100 or more future customers. I've tried to approach my own career with this same dedication to excellence and customer service.

Working on my doctoral degree in engineering was one of the hardest challenges I faced in my life. Academia is a tough, dog-eat-dog environment. Every word, utterance, and equation you present gets challenged and judged on all sides from people who are positive that they're a lot smarter than you. Universities are supposed to be the citadels of openness, tolerance, and awareness, but most of the time these ivory towers are the most caustic, morally destructive, and incomprehensible institutions in America. An old man with a Ph.D. and tenure really does believe he's one of the most intelligent creatures God created, that's if he believes in God, or doesn't think he's God himself.

The saving grace about the field of science or engineering is that at least you can support your conclusions with facts and data. But sometimes facts and data aren't enough to convince the skeptics of your merit, especially when they're unwilling to change or rewrite what they already know. The human mind is complex and the subconscious irrationality of racism, sexism, and classism runs deep, even in our "liberal" universities.

The fact that I graduated from two undergraduate institutions with honors wasn't enough proof for some that I had earned my way into graduate school. Every day was a battle to prove myself — to convince each individual that I belonged in the doctoral program and had every intention of completing it. Many of my colleagues received free passes on exercises and projects, while I was forced to deliver with details and explanations. It was obvious to my peers that I was being tested above and beyond everyone else, but the process made me a stronger individual, and left me with insight and knowledge beyond my years.

There are a couple of hurdles every Ph.D. candidate had to jump over in order to continue in the program. You had to complete an awesome amount of coursework — five to eight hours every night — and maintain a minimum grade point average every semester. The most difficult hurdle of all, the one every engineer with a Ph.D. will reflect upon with horror, was the qualifying exams. These exams were a series of oral and written exams given on several subject areas over a period of a couple of days. My qualifiers consisted of written and oral exams in three areas of mechanical engineering. The two-hour written exams occurred during one week with the 30-minute to one-hour oral exams administered during the following week.

Just the thought of these exams would tie my stomach in knots. For nearly ten hours a day for six months I studied for these exams. Whether I was watching "The Cosby Show" or cheering for the Atlanta Braves during the World Series, I would always have a book and notes before me, sitting at my kitchen table, which I'd named Qualifiers Station 101. I forced my two roommates to eat their dinners somewhere else, except for Fridays when we threw my books in the corner and participated in cut-throat domino games until the wee hours of the morning.

The qualifiers always occurred at the end of October or the beginning of November so that the test takers received the score in time to re-enroll for the winter quarter beginning in January. You could pass any exam independent of the others or pass all three. In any case, each individual had two opportunities to pass three areas. If you failed a section or two, you could take that part again the next time around. The test and oral exams were administered by a committee of three to four professors selected at department meetings and authorized by a vote of the full engineering faculty.

The closer the exams got, the more "geeked" I became about taking them. I was the first African-American in the history of the Georgia Tech School of Mechanical Engineering to be selected directly into the Ph.D. program from the undergraduate program. This knowledge placed an extra burden on my shoulders. There were many professors who thought I was not Ph.D. quality, and they'd expressed these sentiments to the graduate coordinator for the school of engineering. The coordinator stood his ground and told them that my record stood up against all of the other applicants to the doctoral program.

Eventually, the coordinator felt that I should be aware of the general attitude in the department and shared the professors' sentiments with me. I appreciated his honesty and commitment to me and realized my presence represented a paradigm shift for many in the college. By telling me the real issues, he expressed respect for my intellect and maturity. He felt I could handle this undue pressure, and that I was the right man in the right place at the right time to change the wrong thinking of some people.

The days approaching the exams were excruciating. I couldn't sleep and studied until my eyes watered constantly. I worried about failing the exams and having to retake them, which would require me to do a lion's share of the same studying all over again. Even more fearful was the prospect that I might never pass them and be asked to leave the program, meaning all my work thus far would have been in vain.

The three test areas were heat transfer, fluid mechanics, and thermodynamics. On the first attempt, I passed fluid mechanics and thermodynamics, but failed the heat transfer section. Six months later, I passed the heat transfer portion and gained candidacy into the doctoral program.

With a huge hurdle behind me, I felt relieved, but a larger hurdle remained ahead. The next step in the Ph.D. program was the proposal phase. This is where you have to research a topic of interest for a period of time and write a proposal of work. This proposal must be written according to National Science Foundation standards and submitted in document form. You were required to present the work to the Dissertation Committee with the goal of convincing them that the work was worthy of a doctoral degree. At the end of the day, the committee voted you up to the Ph.D. program or back to the drawing board, seriously delaying your progress toward a doctoral degree.

I thought the qualifying exams were nerve-wracking but the proposal phase scared the bejesus out of me. Having to research a topic, write a document, and defend it before a committee of expert professors was too intimidating to consider.

I remember calling home to talk to my parents one night. My mother could always hear when something wasn't right in my voice. I told her what I was facing and she did her motherly job of trying to console my nerves and calm my fears. As she spoke softly to me, I could hear my father rumbling, mumbling, and rambling in the background. "What's wrong with the boy? What's wrong with him? Give me the phone, let me talk to him!"

My father got on the phone and asked sternly, "What's wrong with you? What's going on?" I told him about having to research, document and present my ideas before the proposal committee. I explained to him that I'd been working three years, and now I was faced with the terrible task of having to defend myself before this board of experts. At the end of the defense, they would either vote to keep me and allow me to continue to work toward my doctoral degree or send me packing immediately.

My father began to laugh as my list of concerns grew longer and my voice began to crack. He said, "Boy, you know I have to deal with that kind of pressure every day. Every time I complete a big job, the project manager sends these educated guys in shirts and ties to inspect the roof. They always explain that they need to look and examine it and may have to cut into it to determine if the job's been performed correctly and up to standards. After looking in every crack and crevice, they usually ask condescendingly, 'Where would you like for us to cut the roof?' I always answer by telling them to pick up a stick, any stick, and throw it over any one of their shoulders. They ask, 'Why should we do that, what's that going to tell us?' and I tell 'em, 'throw the stick over your shoulder and wherever it lands, that's where you cut!'"

> *"The only thing that separates anyone of us from excellence is fear, and the opposite of fear is faith. I am careful not to confuse excellence with perfection. Excellence I can reach for, perfection is God's business."*
>
> – Michael J. Fox[*]

"I've been roofing 40 years and there's no substitute for experience!" he continued. "Because I got experience I'm never worried about where they cut or how they look at the roof. Excellence is a standard for us so it doesn't matter where they cut the roof because excellence is throughout the job. That's my guarantee and that's why I've been in the same business on the same job for 40 years!"

---

[*] Quoted by Lorne A. Adrain in *The Most Important Thing I Know.* New York: Cader Books, 1997. p. 77.

My father didn't let me off the phone that easy. He proceeded to bite deep into me with the ferocity of a rabid dog. "Don't ever be scared of anyone evaluating your work. You've worked hard and long and there'll be no one in that room who knows more about what you've done than you. Invite them to read every word of every sentence of every page of what you've written. If you've worked hard, done your best, and made excellence your standard, then you won't have anything to worry about."

"And I don't ever want to hear you talking like this again, boy," he roared at me. "Because I'll come up there and knock you out if you let those people intimidate you again." I answered meekly that I understood. "Do you understand me? Do you understand?" He was screaming at me. "Point made and taken," I replied.

Whew! I may have been happy to hang up the phone, but I was definitely motivated and my confidence grew with every "Do you understand?" he threw at me. I was ready to take on the world and especially my committee.

In the end, the proposal presentation went off without a hitch and I passed with minor changes to my plan. All my self-doubt and worry was for nothing. I was in control of the situation from day one because I'd properly prepared. I still needed someone to give me reassurance though and my dad in his usual stern way provided the reassurance in the form of a swift kick in the butt. He helped me to realize that everything we do eventually will be evaluated and judged by someone. We shouldn't fear this evaluation, but welcome and encourage it, for it'll ultimately help us improve our weak areas. The important thing is not to focus on the evaluation but on doing your best. Excellence comes from trying your hardest and correcting your mistakes when you fall a little short of perfection.

Fear is the Enemy That Keeps Us From Doing Our Best — Do Not Let It Get the Best of You By Being Unprepared

I once heard someone describe FEAR as "False Experiences Accepted as Real." This acronym implies that we sometimes create dire or bad situations in our heads based on lies, half-truths, and our imagination, despite what might be happening in reality. Ultimately, we usually find or realize that what we feared would happen was not that bad after all.

As human beings, we often take on "the dirty clothes," or bad experiences of others as our own. We observe people going through tremendous personal and professional challenges and struggles without ever questioning how they got there. Because a journey was difficult for someone else doesn't mean it has to be as intense a journey for you. Examine other people's paths, habits, and preparations before accepting their fates as your own. The wise man learns from the mistakes of others and he watches what others do and operates differently, depending on the outcome. Likewise you must seek and learn, but do not mimic. Use the struggles and challenges others face as stepping stones to making the journey easier for you.

I always look for so-called successful and unsuccessful people to talk to any chance I get. I believe I can learn from anyone, especially those that have gone before me in similar situations in which I find myself. I may follow them, but that doesn't mean I prescribe to their destiny, be it good or bad. I recognize that I am on a personal journey and must face challenges and tribulations with the unique intellect and experiences I have and have gone through in this short life.

145

My intellect is partly shaped by the experience of others. Why not? There are other people in the world who definitely have more experience and knowledge than I in certain areas. Why shouldn't I learn from them? Share in their wisdom? This is exactly why mentors and mentoring are so important. We should seek to avoid making the mistakes of our ancestors, while pushing the boundaries of human experience and goodness unencumbered by fear, especially fear of the unknown.

Preparation and hard work are the characteristics needed to combat the anxiety of fear. Often when the future is before us, we become paralyzed by what may or may not happen. We have to prepare for the future and understand that we actually can shape our destiny. Man often fears shaping his destiny, thus leaving a lot to chance so he doesn't have to take responsibility for what he created.

I don't know about you, but I want my hands on the steering wheel of my life. On many occasions, fear has caused my chest to pound like someone was trying to jumpstart me. A long time ago, I realized the best way to conquer this fear was to prepare for the moment and hit it head on. I was deathly afraid of my qualifier exams, but confidence gave me the strength to walk into that room and perform. I knew I had covered my bases and studied the subject matter completely and to the best of my ability. Being prepared didn't ensure a passing mark, but it did give me the confidence and ability to stand for the test. Even though I failed one section, I knew what I had to do to be better prepared for the next time around.

Whether you're doing your homework, writing a book, or creating a presentation or speech, you should expect and seek out evaluation. The critical evaluation of others will help you prepare for the unexpected — those situations or judgments you might have overlooked in your work. Let the feedback from others steer you in the right direction and help you cover all of your bases. Let other people's insights give you a better view of your own strengths and weaknesses. Once you're properly and completely prepared, you can rest assured that you have nothing to fear. The only remaining step is to execute the game plan and perform as expected.

There's a story I often read that encompasses everything I'm trying to say about fear and preparation. The story is called "When the Wind Blows" and it reads as follows:

WHEN THE WIND BLOWS*

A young man applied for a job as a farmhand. When the farmer asked for his qualifications, he said, "I can sleep when the wind blows." This puzzled the farmer. But he liked the young man, and hired him.

A few days later, the farmer and his wife were awakened in the night by a violent storm. They quickly began to check things out to see if all was secure. They found that the shutters of the farmhouse had been securely fastened. A good supply of logs had been set next to the fireplace. The young man slept soundly.

The farmer and his wife then inspected their property. They found that the farm tools had been placed in the storage shed, safe from the elements. The tractor had been moved into the garage. The barn was properly locked. Even the animals were calm. All was well.

---

* Author Unknown. Adapted from Albert L. Zobell Jr.'s *Storyteller's Scrapbook*. Utah: Bookcraft SLC, 1948. pg. 111.

The farmer then understood the meaning of the young man's words, "I can sleep when the wind blows." Because the farmhand did his work loyally and faithfully when the skies were clear, he was prepared for the storm when it broke. So when the wind blew, he was not afraid. He was fearless. He could sleep in peace.

When the wind blows, will you be prepared and fearless like the young man described in the story, or will you fear the outcome of the storm?

In New Orleans, Louisiana, where I was born and raised, this story is more literal than not. It really hits home with me, especially since our city, and my home, rest smack dab in the middle of hurricane alley.

The summer and fall of 2004 turned out to be one of the worst hurricane seasons on record. Shockingly, three different major hurricanes — Frances, Charley, and Ivan — pummeled the state of Florida from three different angles. They reaped untold billions of dollars in damage to the state of Florida, and left thousands of people homeless and without electricity.

Living in New Orleans is almost like inviting disaster because it's the only city on the Gulf of Mexico coast completely below sea level. New Orleans, surrounded by water on all three sides, is kept artificially dry by levees, dikes, and manmade pumps. The Federal Emergency Management Agency estimates from scientific models that if the city of New Orleans took a direct hit from a Category Three or above hurricane, the city would see storm surges of 15 to 25 feet. The storm would push water up the mouth of the Mississippi River into Lake Pontchartrain, causing massive flooding in the crescent bowl area that is New Orleans. All models predict such a scenario would place New Orleans under 20 feet of water lasting at least four to six months and causing between 10,000 and 50,000 deaths. I take these hurricanes and the possible catastrophic effects very seriously.

In 2001, residents evacuated as a Category Three hurricane had the city in its cross hairs. Most recently in 2004, the danger was even worse as hurricane Ivan, a Category Five monster, headed directly for New Orleans.

As a father with an infant son, I knew I had to be prepared for the worst. My house has twin, six by eight feet clear pane windows facing each other in the front and in the back. As an engineer, I know if I lose one of those windows in a major storm I lose my entire house. So during the spring, I ordered hurricane storm shutters for the windows and doors on my home and in hindsight, and it was a good thing that I did.

Three days before Ivan's predicted landfall, the mayor ordered an evacuation of the entire city. I called my brother, Willie, and my cousin, Lawrence, to help me install the storm shutters. We worked all day placing the corrugated metal protectors in place and I spent the rest of the evening moving some items upstairs out of path of possible floodwaters. I collected and packed important papers, collectibles, and computers and loaded the truck. Meanwhile my wife packed clothes and prepared the baby for the trip. I thanked my brother and cousin and we discussed different evacuation routes and agreed that it would be best to leave in the middle of night to avoid the reported miles of bumper-to-bumper evacuation traffic.

Like a thief in the night, we departed at 3 AM heading west and then north into Mississippi. My brother, sisters, and I were in communication throughout the night via cell phone making sure everyone was safe and awake. When I arrived at our evacuation location, I checked to make sure that my family members all had made it to their intended locations. Instantly, my mind fastened on Lawrence who had helped me prepare for the storm. I hadn't heard from him yet. I eventually reached him on his cell phone and he told me he'd decided to stay put and that he'd be okay. I listened and wished him well before asking him what his plan would be if the storm came. He replied that if the storm came, he would take his daughter and move downtown to a hotel. It sounded good to him, but I explained that he and his daughter would have to flee their house facing hurricane winds and possible floodwaters with no guarantee of securing a place at the hotel. Furthermore, I informed him that the city keeps over 10,000 body bags for such catastrophic events and had an additional 50,000 bags on order in case of a direct hit from hurricane Ivan. I said that his lack of planning and foresight made it all the more possible that two of those bags would be reserved for both him and his daughter.

We laugh about his decision and the storm now, but it was no joke at the time. My cousin is a grown man and could take care of himself, but his daughter deserved better. By failing to plan effectively, he was, as some old people like to say, planning to fail. Lucky for him, God was watching out for them both.

That night the wind blew very hard in New Orleans and my cousin Lawrence didn't get much sleep as he worried about his safety. My family, on the other hand, slept very well, for we were prepared and out of possible harm's way. Like the young man in the story, we slept in peace as the wind blew and were fearless because we were prepared.

Four Ways to Overcome the Fear of Evaluation

Fear is one of the strongest forces known to humankind and has been known to paralyze people. When we don't face our fears, the power of the fear actually grows. It becomes the ghost or boogey man in the closet — the phantom who won't allow us to live up to our fullest potential.

Many people hold themselves back from doing their best because they're afraid of evaluation. To master your potential and develop the courage to overcome fear, we must take proactive steps in our lives. As leadership expert John C. Maxwell says, your attitude and potential go hand in hand.* Therefore, we must work to make sure that we have the right attitude to succeed and overcome our most inner and deeply held fears. Developing the right mindset to produce the right outcomes requires daily effort and awareness. Every day commit to doing the following:

1 Master your craft

Theodore Roosevelt said, "Whenever you are asked if you can do a job, tell 'em, 'Certainly, I can!' Then get busy and find out how to do it." Learning and mastering your craft is not a static or linear process. Mastery is dynamic as your craft is forever changing and growing. You must change and grow with the knowledge base required to serve the craft. Lifelong learning must exist as one of your core values. Mastering your craft will give others the permission and freedom to pursue their greatest potential also. Set your goals for mastery higher than the standards of the profession. And always remember, this journey toward mastery

---

* John C. Maxwell. *Attitude 101.* Nashville: Thomas Nelson Publishers, 2003. p. 13.

151

must be personal and consistent. Enough is not good enough anymore because the person who outthinks you rules you, and the person who outworks you beats you.

2 Be prepared

Always be prepared for the unexpected. Understand that you have the right to fail, but take pains to ensure you'll never be surprised.

When you're the captain of the ship, it's your responsibility to have the crew prepared for any type of storm. What you try may not work, but no one should ever be able to say that you didn't have a plan. When you've mastered your craft, preparation is a logical step to achieving excellence. Make the plan and then work the plan! My father would intently watch the weather every night to plan the work for the next day. He refused to be caught off guard by nature and did everything possible to avoid such a pitfall. Success and failure often may be tracked back to your preparation for the task.

3 Don't take anything personally

As published in my *Success Manifesto,* keep in mind that "it isn't always about you!" Taking everything personally is the most basic demonstration of selfishness. Another person's comments or insults derive from his or her own attitudes, insecurities, beliefs, and opinions. Refuse to accept another individual's emotional and personal baggage. The psychological defense mechanism known as "projection" refers to what happens when we screen onto others that which we see in ourselves. It's for that reason we can't accept and internalize criticism. When someone rejects what you're selling or the work you've written, they're not rejecting you. When you're attempting to achieve greatness or become great, your thoughts and ideas will be rightfully challenged and scrutinized. Don't take scrutiny as a personal affront to your intelligence or abilities. Accept the criticism for what it really is: a constructive opportunity to learn, grow, and improve or a destructive manifestation of the insecurity, envy, or shortsightedness of someone else. With experience, you'll readily learn the difference between the two.

4 Commit to excellence

Commit to excellence in everything that you do and refuse to settle for anything less than the best from within your circle of existence, including yourself. When excellence becomes an attitude, evaluation and the results become a foregone conclusion where all that remains is the energy and effort required for the commitment. Fear not, for you know that your work and effort meets all standards.

> *"Work hard so God says to you 'Well Done.' Be a good workman, one who does not need to be ashamed when God examines your work."*
> — II Timothy 2:15

WILLIE'S VIEW

Once I knew that I wanted to have a career in the restaurant industry, I did everything I could to learn all there was to know about it. Along the way, I worked with some of the giants in the industry and learned a considerable amount more about my place in this business.

Before I went into fine dining as a career choice, I took a job in the hellacious world of fast foods. The company I worked for had 12 stores at that time and was growing rapidly. I was hired as an Assistant Manager and quickly worked my way up to General Manager.

When I signed my contract, I was ready for the long haul. There was only one thing I didn't want, and that was to be put in this one store in this one part of town. Everyone knew it was a slum store in a slum neighborhood and no one in the company wanted to work it. So guess which store I got sent to?

Everything about this place was wrong. The crew stole everything that didn't move. All the equipment was broken. The roof leaked. To make matters worse, we went through managers at this store like a dart through a balloon at the county fair.

Before I walked into that store I'd armed myself with the most thorough knowledge of all the policies and procedures that came with the job. When I entered the door of that restaurant I noticed not one policy was being enforced. I was going to change that. I called a meeting of the full crew and told them how things were going to change. We would only do what the procedure manual called for with no exceptions.

To make a statement like that you had to be well versed on procedure, so every day I studied something new and applied it. I walked in knowing the procedure manual like the back of my hand. I was determined to know it like the front.

Like every job, we lost a great deal of the crew, but those who stayed noticed a tremendous difference in the way things were going. Customers started asking for me to let me know how pleased they were with the new attitudes of the staff, and our profits and losses started to balance out. I ordered new uniforms, cleaned up around the outside, added a coat of paint to the place, and before you knew it, we were back in business. Because we went back to the basics, my team knew what to expect each and every day and it made things a lot more pleasant for them.

One day my supervisor called and said that we'd be rolling out a new product and soon I'd be getting it, along with the specs, delivered to my store. A training crew, which consisted of the vice president of the company, our local trainer, and my supervisor, would go around to each store to roll the new product out. When I looked at the training schedule I notice that my store was last to get the training. I knew what this meant. Because of our previous bad rep we were the redheaded stepchildren of the bunch.

I'd worked too hard getting my crew to take pride in their work and place of business. I couldn't let them know how we were being treated. So I went home, studied all the specs and procedures of this new product and came back to work ready to roll it out on my own.

The day finally came for the training crew to pay us a visit. I didn't tell the crew that the team was there to roll out the new product. I said it was an inspection and we had to be ready. The store was spotless, everyone was in a new uniform, and the new product was flying out the window. When the team walked in, my supervisor looked at me and I smiled and turned away. I know I wasn't supposed to be selling that product, but this was my only chance to show them that I was one of the best managers they had. They were so impressed that they really did do an inspection that day and we passed with flying colors.

After that visit, my store was given a full face-lift and was used as a training store for managers. I got a promotion as training manager and I did the sexual harassment seminars for the downtown area of New Orleans.

My success here was not by accident. Remember the story of the inspectors coming on to one of my dad's roofs with their books and suits to inspect his work? When they'd ask him where he'd like for them to start, he'd hand them a stick and say, "Just turn around and throw this stick over you shoulder. Wherever it lands is where you should start." This is the exact feeling I had when they came to my restaurant: "Look around wherever you want. I'm sure whatever you find will be just like in your manual."

There Will Always Be Hard Times: Prepare!

When it Rains, It Pours

When changing or repairing a roof, you always have to be cognizant of the weather. If you don't know what the weather will be, you might wind up removing the roof only to have the rain come and do more damage to the building than if you hadn't attempted to fix things in the first place. The weather is always in the forefront of the roofer's mind.

My father loved Clint Eastwood westerns such as *The Good, The Bad and The Ugly* and TV shows like "Gunsmoke." Growing up, it seemed like my father would find a western movie or show to watch every night, but as soon as the program ended, we had to immediately turn the television to the news. It didn't matter how exhausted he was, my father had to stay awake to watch the weather. Even if he fell asleep, he would always make sure to put one of us in charge of waking him up when it was time for tomorrow's forecast. His obsession made perfect sense: He had to see the weather to determine how he would plan for his next workday. This was long before the luxuries of the Internet, the Weather Channel, and the 24 hour news cycle.

My father would watch the weather and make comments like he was the weatherman. After being outside on the roof for nearly 40 years, he had become skilled at predicting trends and patterns for himself. He had his own mechanisms for determining and gauging how the weather might change on a dime. Whether there was a prediction for afternoon thunder storms, morning showers, or hot, hazy sun, he knew what each forecast really meant for his business, and what he had to do on site the next day to maximize the work output of his crew. He never let a weatherman's poor prediction catch him by surprise.

My father would seem to know exactly how much roof we had to remove in order to replace it before the rain came. The funny thing was, he always knew the rain would come. It always comes in New Orleans, especially in the afternoon. Sometimes afternoon thundershowers will almost flood the city in a matter of minutes, and then the sun will slide out from behind the clouds as if the rain had never happened.

With an afternoon shower almost always guaranteed, my father wasted no time getting us to work. As soon as we climbed on the roof, he would begin barking out cadence like a drill sergeant. He'd give measurements, direct the delivery truck, call out the temperature for the asphalt operator, direct the supply lines, all while keeping an eye on his wristwatch and the horizon. Often, he would just stand upright in the middle of working and stare intensely into the sky. At times, with unbelievable urgency, he would just begin screaming, pushing everyone to work harder and faster because the rain was coming. Looking into the sky, we'd see nothing but blue patches with white cumulus clouds, and think to ourselves that he was crazy. Then sure enough two or three hours later, like clockwork, an ominous darkness would appear. My father would point it out and say, "I told you the rain would come!"

But even the best weathermen sometimes miss an on-coming storm, and my father, unfortunately, was no different. He always warned me that the rain would come. I vividly remember the first time I saw the rain come into his life, and it caught him unprepared.

"Pleasant experiences make life delightful.
Painful experiences lead to growth."
— Anthony de Mello*

One day I came home and knew things had changed. As soon as I walked through the door, I could feel the tension in the air, so thick you could cut it with a knife. My mother was sitting at the bar, which separated the family room from the kitchen. I still get chills down my spine when I recall the tired look on her face. We didn't exchange any words, but the silence said it all. I immediately began to look for my dad and saw his truck in the driveway.

My dad left home in the mornings before the rest of us got up and returned home late in the evening, dirty after a hard day's work. He usually entered the house, removing his tarred shoes at the kitchen door before moving swiftly upstairs to the shower.

I bounced up the stairs expecting to see him sitting on the side of his king-sized brass bed. He wasn't there so I entered the master suite bathroom, and there was still no sign of him. Something drew me to the bedroom window overlooking the backyard, and looking out I saw him standing in the backyard looking up toward the stars. I'd never seen him so pensive and stoic. I sensed in my heart something was wrong with this picture.

---

* Anthony de Mello. *Awareness: The Perils and Opportunities of Reality.*

I turned around, went downstairs, and started to make my way to him in the backyard. As I exited the steel rod back door, he never turned to look to see who was there, he just blurted out in a dry distant voice, "Boy, what do you want?" I responded, "I came to see what you're doing." He didn't say anything, so I just stood there looking at his back as he puffed one of his unfiltered Camel cigarettes, which he still smokes to this day.

Then he said, "I'm thinking about blowing my brains out." I asked, "Why would you do that?" He said, "Because right now I'm worth more dead!" Puzzled I just stood there running back these crazy thoughts through my head. "Daddy, what're you talking about?" "You'll find out," he said, "real soon."

I returned back to the kitchen where my mother sat, looking pensive with introspection. "What's going on?" I asked her. She looked at me and said that the Internal Revenue Service had shut the business down and frozen all of their bank accounts. My knees became weak as the seriousness of the situation sunk in. I asked my mother what we were going to do, and with her eyes welling up with tears she mumbled, "I don't know." This was definitely the rain my father had predicted.

I went back outside and sat at the patio table a couple of feet from where my father was standing. He began to describe his entire life to me. He talked about growing up with nothing, how he was not privy to an education, how he worked hard every day to provide for his family and damn, now this. He was afraid he was going to lose everything he had worked for and built over time.

I was afraid to probe him on the business issue, but tried to reassure him that everything would be okay. He asked me some simple questions. He said, "Do you have a mortgage? Do you have a car note? Do you pay your tuition? Do you pay the utilities or buy the food in this house?" I answered "No" to each one of these questions. Then he asked, "How in hell do you know it'll be okay?"

I didn't answer and this was the first time I had ever heard an expression of doubt coming from my father's lips. This was the first time I heard him question himself and it was definitely the first I saw him unprepared for the rain.

He and his brother had built a commercial roofing and supply company that employed at its peak over 100 men. They were supplying roofing material for the construction of entire subdivisions. Mackie Roofing was winning government contracts to waterproof and re-roof federal, state, and local government buildings. They were subcontractors on larger private construction projects.

Two country boys from St. Francisville, Louisiana had been true to themselves and built a business that actually stabilized a community in New Orleans. Many of the young men who worked at the business lived in the community and otherwise had no other skills. Mackie Roofing gave them incredible opportunities by introducing them to the construction and contracting business and teaching them a skilled trade. Still to this day, many roofers can trace their beginnings to the training they received from my father.

As I later found out, the Internal Revenue Service shut the business down and froze the accounts primarily because of unpaid taxes. The IRS probe revealed many glaring irregularities in how the company handled its taxes. Moreover, sheer evidence of theft emerged from the investigations, and all of it could be traced back to the misdeeds of a few trusted employees — employees my father had trained, and to whom he had given responsibilities and opportunities they never would have received anywhere else.

As trusting hardworking individuals, my father and uncle had taken their eyes off of the ball and left important financial responsibilities to individuals without proper regard for checks and balances. My father believed in people and it came back to bite him in the behind. This event was the ultimate display of disrespect to him because he not only trusted the people who betrayed him, but he counted them as a part of his family. He had known these guys since they were teenagers. He gave them more than they ever had in their lives and they still stole from him.

For the first time in his life, my father had not prepared for the rain. He was caught with the roof wide open and the rain was now pouring down in the gaping hole. I guess the only hole that was bigger was the one in his heart. The damage he experienced went much deeper than his own family, as all of his employees were left without a job or a way to support their families. My father felt the weight of the world on his shoulders. He knew he had to face everyone and tell them he had nothing for them. He had to explain to them why he had not prepared for this storm.

Eventually the company began to operate again and generate funds to pay the IRS and support my father and uncle. Eventually they were both able to hire many of those same employees back again. But the hit from the IRS was a big blow, and the company has never been able to return to the glory days of performing large-scale commercial work. The rain left some permanent damage behind in its wake, and to this day my father is still haunted by what he could have done to be more prepared. He is a changed man because of it — one who now accepts responsibility for all aspects of his business.

Prepare for the rain because the sun won't shine forever

Rain is the roofer's blessing and curse. It giveth work, and it taketh work away. On the one hand, if there were no such thing as rain, then roofers would be out of a profession because the tops of houses wouldn't get damaged and leak. On the other hand, if roofers don't respect the power and mystery of nature by properly preparing to deal with the rain, it can also be their kryptonite.

At any moment the rain can destroy everything you attempt to build and create. Many a roofer has lost everything by having a building or home exposed with no roof when the rain arrived. For this reason, my father always taught us to respect the rain. It occupied many of our discussions on the roof and at the dinner table. It provided food and shelter for us for many years.

In life, as in roofing, the rain will eventually come and all of us must be prepared. Recently, I was speaking at a university to an audience of about 3,000 students, and I felt really good about the presentation. I got a positive response and lots of students approached me after to talk. When everyone had filed out, the Student Government Association members and I headed to lunch in the President's Dining Hall. We were walking across campus when I saw this young man approaching. I'm very aware of people and their behaviors when I'm speaking in different places, and I remembered noticing this young man sitting in the audience during my speech. I could see from the expression on his face he had something on his mind.

As he got closer he said, "Excuse me, Dr. Mackie, may I speak with you?" I looked at my hosts, asked if I had five minutes to speak with the student, and they said yes. I told them to excuse me and asked the young man what I could do for him.

He said, "Man, I heard your speech and you said some good things, real good things, and I would even say powerful things. But Dr. Mackie, I know how to deal with the sunny days; it's the rainy days I need help with. I've had sunny days, but lately I've been having a lot of rainy days. Dr. Mackie, how do I deal with the rain?"

This question blew me away because this is what my father had been telling me all my life: "the rain will come." I realized at that moment my father wasn't just talking about roofing and weather; he was talking about everyday life for every human being.

I don't care if you're rich, poor, white, black, smart, or dumb, you will have those days that make you question not only yourself, but your very existence as well. This young man was presently facing those types of days. My speech had given him the hope to go on but he felt compelled to seek out more specifics.

I asked him where he would be in two hours and he said, "Wherever you want me to be." I told him to meet me in the student union where we met and talked for hours. As the conversation ended and he was about to depart, I told him never to forget that regardless of how sunny it may be, "the rain will come and we must prepare for it. The rain will come, but the sun must eventually shine."

My father joked about blowing his brains out because he hadn't prepared himself for the possibilities that arose from the IRS audit. Although he warned me that the rain would come, he actually thought the sun would always shine for him. Many of us get lulled into the same false sense of financial and physical security, which causes us to believe the sun will shine upon us all the time. Many of us are able to face and overcome professional adversities except those of our own making.

Between 1992 and 2000, the country experienced the greatest economic expansion in the history of the world. Many individuals thought the stock market would grow forever. Stock options were being handed out like candy on Halloween, and jobs were as plentiful as those lonely *USA Today* sport sections I see left behind in airports. The good times were rolling, and we thought they'd roll forever.

Over that period people spent like crazy. They didn't save for the day when the rain would come. In the year 2000, the rain finally came, and in a big way. People are still trying to recover from their losses, as personal and national debts continue to soar four years later. People are struggling to hold on to their present jobs, and economic fear is driving us to be even more individualistic and self-centered at work. As a nation, we no longer teach people to have an umbrella ready for a rainy day, or how to prepare for tomorrow.

"The rain will come." My father taught me this adage in the most poignant way: He lived it. On the brink of financial ruin, he had to make some serious decisions. He had to reach deep within and grasp for a part of his soul and spirit that hadn't been awakened in a while. His success had lulled him into a deep sense of comfort and complacency that was rudely interrupted by the reality of the rain. He made the joke about blowing out his brains because, he said, a weaker man would've actually done so. He talked about how rich men when faced with financial ruin often killed themselves, like the stock brokers who jumped out of the windows on Wall Street during the Crash of 1929.

One evening, while sipping on a beer and watching Monday night football, he made a statement that let me know everything would be okay. He simply said that he had no other choice but to get up each morning and go make it right. He said that he had done it once and could do it all again. He knew what it felt like to have nothing, so he wasn't afraid of starting from nothing. He was committed to duplicating his success.

In the end, my father saved his business. He was able to continue to take care of his family and still provide opportunities for other men and their families. Through his adversity and subsequent victory, my father taught me that you have to prepare for the rain because the sun won't shine forever.

Five Areas to Prepare For When the Rain Comes

When the rain comes, we have to be prepared. There are five areas of our life in which we should spend some time every day preparing: Mental Awareness, Education, Ethnicity, Finances, and Health.

1 Mental Awareness (Consciousness and Spirituality)

Regardless of what you call it, consciousness or spirituality, we have to strengthen our mental awareness every day. Mental awareness is the vehicle that leads us down the path to truth.

"There is in this world no such force as the force of a man determined to rise. The human soul cannot be permanently chained."
— W.E.B. DuBois

The philosopher Bertrand Russell said, "Many people would sooner die than think; in fact, they do so." Our ability to think and our mental consciousness separates us from other creatures in God's world. Everything in the universe can be placed into four categories, either as a mineral, a plant, an animal, or a human being. Furthermore, everything in the universe consists of the same substances in rudimentary states: hydrogen, oxygen, and carbon, with some trace elements. If I take a rock and pulverize it, we'll find dust consisting of hydrogen, oxygen, and carbon. If we take a vegetable and pulverize it, we again will find those same three elements. If we take samples of animals and humans and pulverize them, again we would find hydrogen, oxygen, and carbon.

As humans, we know we're not minerals, animals, or vegetables, but we're still the same at some level. So we have to ask ourselves, what makes us different? The answer is: our level of awareness, consciousness, or spirituality. I'm not talking about religion, although religion is a vehicle used by many individuals to achieve a greater consciousness or spirituality. (Someone once told me that religion is for people who are scared to go to hell; spirituality is for people who have already been there.) You have to understand that there is something greater in you — something that gives you breath every day — which separates you from minerals, plants, and animals. Spirituality raises us from our purely physical existence and demonstrates that there is a core part of us that can't be pulverized or broken down into common elements.

If properly nourished and cultivated, mental awareness will become the voice within that guides us daily. It will help us separate truth and wisdom from fear and doubt. My grandmother was the wisest person I ever knew, even though she had never attended a day of school in her life. She just knew the truth. Even tripping over a crack could trigger one of her wisdom nuggets: "See that crack there in the sidewalk, boy?" she'd say. "Don't let the cracks in life trip you up like that." Her awareness and relationship to life and the universe were almost one. She radiated wisdom.

Truth and wisdom must come from within. They must be sought out and awakened. Many of us never do the thinking or meditation necessary to go deeper within ourselves. We have found false security in the education we receive from formal schooling. The world is filled with fear, doubt, jealousy, anger, rage, vengefulness, powerlessness, hatred, envy, inferiority, superiority, greed, and lust because we are detached from our inner awareness and consciousness.

Research has shown that people who pray or meditate have better health than those who don't, and that prayer and meditation have healing powers for those who are sick. Prayer and meditation cause people to be less depressed. Prepare your mental and spiritual self for when the rain comes. It will be a source of strength for you when all else fails.

2 Education (Training and Profession)

I've said it before, and I'll say it again until I'm blue in the face: We must be concerned with life long learning. The world is forever changing and our skills must be updated to maintain our place and value in the market.

The world is dividing itself into two categories: those in the know and those not in the know. The so-called "Knowledge Economy" is placing a premium on our ability to think and solve problems. Formal education is a must for those who want to participate in the present and future knowledge economy. Many of us have fallen victim to the swap meet mentality of education that holds that if you're educated with a degree then somebody owes you a job or position. We're all aware that jobs are being outsourced from America. This trend won't stop as labor markets continue to develop overseas in rising nations like China and India. Human capital is being developed around the world and we must put ourselves in the place to compete from an intellectual perspective. We have to develop the mentality that our knowledge places us in a position not to swap, but to create positions and create the future. That is the promise of America.

Every one of us has to participate in life long learning and personal development. Master your craft and update your skills continuously so you can maintain a consistent market value for yourself when the rain comes.

3 Ethnicity (Culture and Diversity)

The world is becoming smaller. We must learn, understand, and be prepared to deal with people from other cultures.

In the past, Americans could stick their heads in the ground like ostriches and ignore the rest of the world. Not any more. Americans must now work to become more worldly and tolerant of people who are not like us. We have to travel internationally, see, experience, and digest the world outside of the continental United States.

Diversity is still an issue in the U.S. due to our auspicious past, with which we have not fully come to grips. America and many of her citizens refuse to acknowledge and accept America's history and its relative relationship with minorities from all over the country. History is to a race of people what memory is to a man; when we don't know history and how things came to be, it's like we're functioning with memory loss. That's the reason people can look at the issue of diversity, especially the argument for more of it, and see two different things.

Some people believe that America is a melting pot and everyone should assimilate to be an American. A thought such as this raises the following questions: What is authentically American? Do I have to become more like you to be more American, or you like me? What are we assimilating toward?

America is not a melting pot; it's a tossed salad where all of the ingredients are needed to make a good salad and all the ingredients are acceptable for what they are. The tomatoes remain tomatoes, the onions remain onions, and eggs remain eggs. We shouldn't have to become something else to be considered American. As the world changes, this archaic attitude will continue to stifle growth, development, and productivity in America's workplace and communities.

Author John Henrik Clarke stated: "The events which transpired 5,000 years ago, five years ago or five minutes ago, have determined what will happen five minutes from now, five years from now or 5,000 years from now. All history is a current event."* In order to be more accepting and properly deal with diversity, Americans must continue to study history and ascertain all lessons which have brought us and the world to this point.

---

* This quote is widely known, but I can't locate the source.

4 Finances (Money and Spending)

I believe that if you study spirituality, diversity, and ethnicity, if you get the training and practice of lifelong learning, and if you pursue your dreams with all the zeal, zest, and intestinal fortitude that God has put within you, money will come your way. But once you have money, you have to know how to keep it and make it grow. We have to save and prepare to leave an inheritance for the future generations.

Personal finances are very important and Americans have to be more cognizant of how we spend our money. We are now a debtor nation with more of us going more in debt each day. For the first time in America we are faced with the possibility that this generation will be financially worse off than its parents. Consumerism and unmitigated materialism are robbing us of America's promise — the promise to be free to create wealth and pass it on to our children. More Americans are now more obsessed with looking wealthy than actually doing the tough work of creating wealth. We must study personal finances and do a better job of controlling our spending habits. Prepare your finances for when the rain comes. My father trusted other people to put his personal finances in order, and they failed him. If he had learned how to do it himself, he wouldn't have been as stressed when the rain came.

Some quick tips to improve personal finances are:

- Save and invest a minimum of 10% of your after tax income — $10 for every $100 you make.

- Pay off all bad debt like credit cards. Don't buy anything new until all your other debts are paid.

- Start a program for retirement planning. If your company does not have a 401k program, start what's known as an IRA, which will allow you to save a certain amount per year tax-free.

- Commit to a program of long-term investing with disciplined time intervals. Commit to saving a fixed amount in some financial vehicle like a mutual fund on a regular basis. Ten years ago I began a Direct Re-Invest Program (DRIP) account with Home Depot and McDonald's. Each month $50 was automatically sent to these account to purchase shares (or partial shares) of stocks in these companies. In the beginning, it didn't seem like much, but over time the money has produced a nice nest egg that continues to grow. You can attempt to do the same systematic building through a mutual fund; however, companies such as Disney, Coca-Cola, and Home Depot among others have programs established so that individuals can invest directly into the companies and bypass stockbroker fees.

- Minimize purchasing and spending on items, which depreciate in value such as cars, furniture, electronics, and appliances. Put your money in stocks, bonds, and mutual funds, or buy real estate that will appreciate over time.

- Commit to increasing your personal net worth. You can do this by getting the training and education you need to become a highly-valued specialist in your field, by starting your own business where the potential to earn is limitless, or by getting a second job.

5 Health (Wellness and Well-Being)

. . . .

> *"He who is taught to live upon little owes*
> *more to his father's wisdom than he who has a*
> *great deal left him does to his father's care."*
> — William Penn

. . . .

When the rain comes, our first reaction will be to feel stressed, and stress, as more scientists are starting to point out, can lead to disease and sickness. When the body is under stress it excretes several hormones and other chemicals meant to prepare the body to tackle imposing challenges. It is the imbalance or over-use of this ability that produces wear and tear on the body and functions. Stress is an inevitable part of our daily lives and can be managed effectively by employing coping mechanisms like going to the gym, relaxing, and meditating. If your health is not up to standard, you may suffer more than necessary. Exercise, drink lots of water, stretch, and do all things in moderation. The body is an awesome machine with the capability of repairing itself with proper rest and nourishment.

Become aware of family history and concern yourself with possible predispositions for certain illnesses based on that history. You don't want to exacerbate the possibility of being ill by also being ignorant of your family history and relationship to illness.

A big part of wellness and health has to do with our ability to communicate. We have to learn to let go and express what we're experiencing or feeling inside. We can readily do this by finding accountability partners or individuals we know we can trust to be there and listen to us. There was a study that found women live longer than men for three main reasons:

1. A woman will cry.
2. A woman will tell a friend her problems.
3. A woman will give her problems to God.

We men have not learned nor allowed ourselves to express or properly funnel our feelings so as to avoid additional stress tensors in our lives. Keep a journal, find a friend, or go to a therapist; find a way to express the troubling things in your life. I don't know if my father ever had such avenues and the experience with his business probably has taken years off of his life.

Some promises we should make to ourselves to be better prepared for the rain:

• Exercise regularly. Run, walk or jog.
• Eat healthy. Eat more raw and less processed foods.
• Express yourself verbally or through the written word. Keep a journal.
• Simplify and organize your life. Strive for balance.
• Have fun. Find a hobby you really enjoy and can do for a lifetime, such as fishing or golfing.

WILLIE'S VIEW

I think hard times are things that, on an emotional level, we never can prepare for. The element of surprise is always present. We set goals and standards to prepare our lives for what will be, but when that time comes everything changes.

Growing up, my family really didn't have much to worry about. My father had laid the groundwork for what was supposed to be our future, and he made sure we were educated. I'd been told over and over about "the rain," but it was always something that went totally over my head. I wouldn't let myself believe that anything bad could ever happen to us. We were on a roller coaster ride, going uphill forever, and it was great.

One summer I came home from college and noticed things weren't as festive as they were when I left. I never really asked any questions about anything concerning my folks, so I just let it be. But one day my dad came home early from work and went into his room to lie down, bypassing his regular routine of relaxing with a beer on the couch. My mother emerged from that room with a frown on her face. I asked her what was wrong and she told me that my dad had been having problems with his stomach and wouldn't go to the doctor. This had been going on for some time. When I asked her why she hadn't said anything, she said she didn't want to worry me because I was in school.

I went to my dad's room and asked him if he was alright. He was bundled up in the covers lying in his bed. He looked at me and assured me that he was fine, but I could see from the look on his face that he was in a lot of pain. I knew he was too proud to admit he was hurting, so I just shut the door and let him rest.

At the end of the week my dad's condition worsened. He was now in excruciating pain and could do nothing about it. My mother asked me if I would go with her to take my dad to the hospital. Before we left, my mother made sure that she had all the necessary insurance cards the hospital would need.

I realized quickly this was not just a stomachache. He moaned the whole way there. That five-minute drive seemed like it took an hour. I felt so helpless. My mother was sitting beside me with a frightened look on her face and I could tell she was scared and there was nothing I could do to calm her.

When we got to the hospital, they immediately took my dad into the emergency room. My mom followed. When she returned, she went to the office to give them the insurance information they would need to admit my dad.

A while later she came to me from the office. She was extremely emotional and was shaking something awful. I remember wanting to run out of the hospital thinking my dad had died or something. My mom looked at me and said that the hospital needed $1500 to admit my dad because the insurance had lapsed. My dad lay sick on a hospital gurney, and my mom was in total shock by the news she'd just received.

My mom got the money and my dad was treated and released a couple of days later. His recovery period was filled with questions about his insurance and why it had lapsed. The amazing part of all this was that now the cat was out of the bag and I mean in a huge way.

Upon further investigation, we learned that not only did the hospital insurance lapse, but there were questions about the house, car, and life insurance policies. This wasn't the rain my father spoke so matter-of-factly about, this was the storm. And it wasn't going to let up. For the first time in my life I had to face the fact that the roller coaster was on its way down and there wasn't another hill in sight.

I don't think that all the money in the world could offer you health, and without health, all your goals and strategies are no more than a pipe dream.

I never want my loved ones to be put in the position my mother was in that night. She did everything she could to insure that she would get that money. She didn't feel she was losing her spouse, she felt she was losing her life, and she wasn't going to let that happen.

Today I make sure that my health and life insurance are up to date. Even if I lose everything else, I'll always have tomorrow.

Masters Teach: Passing on Your Knowledge & Mentoring

Cruise Control

There wasn't anything comparable to waking up every Saturday morning and going to work with my father. Riding in the truck's rear bed, holding onto the ladder overhead, listening to men tell their stories about their wild weekends and how "low down" my father was — these were all priceless experiences for me growing up.

Often my father would first go to the warehouse and direct the crews out to different job sites. He'd give them stern instructions followed by the threat that he'd be checking on them throughout the day. This was an ominous warning because if he arrived on a roofing site and people weren't working, or worse, he felt they weren't working up to their potential, all hell was going to break loose.

I loved going on new jobs and roof repairs with my father. He'd get out of the truck and walk up to the house with pride and confidence. He could often see the problems with the roof from the ground the way a teacher can spot mistakes on a student's test paper from across the room. He'd point out errors in previous work and the deterioration in the present structure that needed repairing. Then he'd direct me to knock on the door of the house and let the resident know that "the roofer" was there.

The homeowner usually came out feeling pretty vulnerable. After all, water was leaking into the home and he or she had no way of knowing if what my dad said was correct or honest. With the clarity and simplicity of a professor, he'd escort the resident around the structure and explain why the roof was leaking. "What is this going to cost me, sir?" was the customer's usual, nervous reply.

After doing some calculations, my father would give the customer a firm and fair price. Then he'd follow it up with the same promise every time: "I always guarantee the roof after installation or repairs. If something's wrong with my workmanship, I will personally come out and correct it." These words of assurance usually sealed the deal, and the customer would sign the contact and give my father the okay to start working.

My father taught my brothers and me early on in life that your workmanship and your word are very important. "Be honest and do a good job, and people will call you back and refer you to others," he'd say. "There isn't anything better than a good name, so do everything you can to protect your good name in life and in business." He preached these values and lived them too.

No one went the extra mile for customers like my father. At first, I didn't understand why he freely gave out our home number, so one day I asked him. Sternly he replied, "When you work for yourself and your name is on the business, you're never off work." Sure enough, when the spring and summer months brought daily afternoon showers to New Orleans, our phone would often ring, and like clockwork, my father would answer it, write down some information from the caller, and tell him or her how to stymie the leak to prevent water damage until he arrived. If necessary, he'd bolt from the house directly after the call to satisfy his customers.

"You may not get all that you work for, but you will work for everything that you get."

— Booker T. Washington

It didn't matter how late in the evening a customer called, my father would always respond to an emergency. All he wanted to do when he came home was take a bath, eat, and watch TV. This was his only time to relax. On Monday nights we'd watch Monday Night Football together, and he'd lie in the bed in his undershirt and boxers examining all the aspects of the game. To this day, my father is a big fan of the New Orleans Saints, and if the Saints happen to be playing on Monday night, you'd better believe nothing's going to prevent him from watching every down. But if a customer calls with a leaky roof, my father springs to action, puts on his pants and work boots, and goes back out to the rain and cold. He's lucky to get four or five hours of solid sleep on those long nights.

My father built a reputation and a business by doing excellent work and being on call 24 hours a day, 7 days a week. From his work ethic and efforts, he earned the respect of his colleagues and employees. He didn't expect anyone to do what he wouldn't do himself. He was the consummate teacher and coach, leading others by his example. If you were tired, all you had to do was look over your shoulder, see this man ten to 20 years older than you working continuously, and you knew you had no excuse for slacking off. He believed in making and earning your way in the world. He'd stand outside of his business and watch the trucks come and go and material being bought and sold, and remember when he had just one ladder on top of a car. From the cotton fields to business owner, he earned his success every step of the way with nothing but honesty, dignity, and sweat equity.

Recently, I was waiting at a traffic light when I saw a black Ford F-150 pickup truck covered with magnetic New Orleans Saints helmets cruise across the intersection. Three or four men were riding in the back, and I could see the driver leaning forward over the steering wheel. A smile came to my face. It was my father heading off to work. I made the turn at the intersection and just followed the truck as it barreled its way to a construction site.

The truck continued on for a couple of miles and I eased behind it as it pulled over and came to a rest. Men began jumping from the truck, unloading materials and equipment with haste. Those who recognized me just pointed and made faces knowing that if they stopped for a minute, the drill sergeant would scream.

I exited my car and yelled greetings to Rabbit, Cadillac, Jo-Willie, Pickett, and the other characters we'd made up names for over the years. They walked over, shook my hand, and asked me how things were going. They also let me know that my dad hadn't changed one iota. He was still kicking their collective butts every day. By then, my father had made his way to the rear of the truck and began to tell the men to get on the job.

"Good morning, son," he said reaching out to shake my hand with a smile on his face. "What are you doing up this early?"

"Hell, I gotta work." I told him. "No one's going to give it to me!"

"You damn right about that!" he said.

We both laughed, and then he asked me to excuse him for a minute. "That's okay," I said, "I'm about to leave anyway." "Hell no you don't. Wait a second," he said, walking toward the ladder.

My father climbed onto the roof, and screaming at the top of his voice, directed the men on what to do. After about 15 minutes, he came back down, walked over to me, and began explaining what they were doing to the roof and all of the technicalities that would be involved on the job. Listening intently, I said, "Well I better leave so you can get to work!"

"This is a young man's world. I don't work that hard anymore," my father said. "Sure I can still get on that roof and work all of them to shame, but only if I have to."

"After 40 years, I'm just like you," he continued. "There isn't anything I haven't seen on a roof. I got a Ph.D. in roofing and all I do now is teach. I'm on cruise control like an airplane that just took off. I've reached my altitude, as high as I can go, and all I can do is lie down, cruise, and teach. Now I just answer my phone, make some calls, check jobs, and make sure they're being done right, because these young suckers just don't know how to work…They just don't know anything."

I hung onto my father's every word and admired his sincerity and thoughts. When he finished speaking, I shook his hand again, said goodbye, got back in my car, and drove away. As I pulled out from the curb, I shot a glance to my rearview mirror and saw my father standing there, waving goodbye with one hand, and directing the workers on the roof with the other, like an engaged and masterful teacher.

The Final Test of Every True Master is the Willingness to Teach and Mentor Others

The greatest thing about being a teacher is that you actually touch and shape lives yet unborn. You may influence future presidents, queens, and leaders without ever knowing that your words or instructions inspired this person to great heights. There's no greater profession or responsibility for any person who considers him – or herself – a master at what he or she does.

Everyone has a responsibility to future generations to pass on the knowledge they have attained and inspire others to tackle the problems facing humankind. There's no man alive who wasn't once a boy, and no teacher who wasn't once a student. At a certain level, we're forever students absorbing what this life has to teach and reveal to us. When we stop learning, we stop growing and become a part of the walking, breathing, living dead with no dreams and especially no hope for the future.

Who are your teachers? Who are the people who provide those nerve-calming and settling words, or make the complex seem so simple and the world all right for you? These people are masters who have reached a level of knowledge and understanding, and have recognized their responsibility to educate the next generation of doers, thinkers, and scholars in all areas.

My father has been teaching the roofing profession for 40 years, making sure the profession lives and grows. Beyond teaching, he has taken time to mentor other roofers, coaching them through the process of starting their own roofing business and becoming self-empowered achievers of the so-called "American Dream."

Teaching and mentoring fit together like a hand in a glove. Teaching provides you with the map, but mentoring leads you down the road to your destination. It extends instruction to the point of execution. We all need teaching, but we all need mentoring as well.

Mentoring is a new buzzword in business. Many corporations are beginning to establish formal mentoring networks in an attempt to foster increased success rates among employees, especially for women and minorities. The concept of mentoring, however, is not new.

The term mentor is over 3,000 years old and has its origins in Greek mythology. Greek legend holds that when Odysseus went off to fight in the Trojan War, he left his trusted friend Mentor in charge of his household and the education of his son Telemachus. He asked Mentor to watch over his son and provide him with the education, guidance, and direction he'd give him personally if he didn't have to leave for war. Since then, Mentor's name has been attached to the process of education and care by an older, experienced person. In time, the word Mentor has become synonymous with trusted advisor, friend, and teacher. History offers many examples of helpful mentoring relationships — Socrates and Plato, Hayden and Beethoven, Freud and Jung.

Mentoring is a process of building a mutually beneficial partnership between experienced persons (mentors) and less experienced persons (protégés) to help develop the skills, behaviors, and insights to reach the partnership's goals. Some mentoring relationships are formal, such as the ones that exist between a boss and a young employee. Many organizations in fact have established formal mentoring relationships to confront the gender or race bias inherent in some well-established fields, which lack sufficient role models to serve as mentors for people who may otherwise get left outside of the "good ol' boy" networks. Other mentoring relationships are more casual, such as the natural bonds that often develop between a father and son or an uncle and a nephew.

Mentoring goes to the heart of what drives an organization — its people and its culture — and works best when established naturally and informally. My father took an interest in those who showed an expressed passion for roofing and wanted to establish themselves in the roofing profession. There's an old adage that states, "When the student is ready, the teacher will appear." When my father directed you to meet him somewhere and perform a task in a certain manner, it was evidence of your desire to be taught, mentored, and coached with no strings attached. He expected nothing in return for his time, except that you listened and some day would teach that skill to somebody else.

Most individuals require multiple mentors because it's often impossible to discover everything you need to know from a single person. As you grow older, your needs for development grow too, and you should find mentors who can satisfy your new needs accordingly. My father's teaching and mentoring delivered me to a certain place in life and provided me with a foundation upon which to build. But I needed additional mentors to ultimately help me achieve the career goals I sought to accomplish in life, career goals that were beyond the scope of my father's experience and education.

The role of the mentor

My experiences as both a protégé and a mentor have taught me that a mentor must function in four primary roles: as an advisor, as a networker, as a facilitator, and as a coach. The principal ingredient in all of these roles is communication. If location, location, location is the key to success in real estate, then communication, communication, communication is the key to success in any mentoring relationship. A good mentor must first and foremost be a good communicator, someone who can listen and offer advice without passing judgment.

Mentor as advisor

The mentor shares and gives advice regarding career development within the organization. Depending on the depth of the relationship, the mentor will also provide information regarding personal matters.

In graduate school, I was assigned an advisor, Dr. Prateen Desai, to direct my research and provide guidance toward my doctoral degree. Dr. Desai accepted, challenged, and believed in me as an individual. He never made excuses for my shortcomings, and inspired me to continuously strive for more.

During the second year of our relationship, I won a $5,000 cash scholarship, and due to our relationship and the depth of our discussions beyond engineering and technology, I felt very comfortable asking Dr. Desai how I should save or invest the money. This man of Indian descent directed me to invest the money in a high-quality aggressive mutual fund, something no one in my family had ever done before.

Dr. Desai gave me some information about the fund and left the decision up to me. After studying the recommended material, I invested the money and it turned out to be one of the best decisions I ever made and the best advice I ever received. I was only able to approach him because he felt comfortable sharing a part of himself with me.

I am eternally grateful to Dr. Prateen Desai for his mentorship and advice on all matters. Once he even told me an Indian secret for lowering high blood pressure, which consisted of copper pots and room temperature water. I don't know if the method actually works, but I found it very interesting nevertheless.

Mentor as networker

The mentor helps the protégé build internal and external relationships with important high-level people. These relationships serve as a resource network, which allows the protégé to access necessary information otherwise unavailable. In other words, mentors have a responsibility to bring you into their networks and give you credibility where you otherwise would have none. As a protégé it's your responsibility not to violate their trust and belief in you.

Recently, I ran into Dr. Marshall Jones of General Electric Corporation and a member of the National Academy of Engineering (NAE). After chatting and catching up, I explained that meeting him at this point in my life was like closing a loop.

I had been introduced to Dr. Jones 14 years before at the American Society of Mechanical Engineers Annual Conference in California. The person who introduced us was Dr. Carolyn Meyers, Provost and Vice Chancellor at North Carolina Agriculture and Technical University in Greensboro, North Carolina. Dr. Meyers often allowed me to accompany her to conferences, where she'd introduce me to everyone who might be able to help me in the future. Being a new graduate student and novice at the conference, she told me that Dr. Jones was the person to emulate. I never forgot him and followed his work through the announcements in the trade magazines. Presently, the two of us are visiting professors at the University of Michigan, but our first formal introduction happened because of Dr. Meyers, and I'm still grateful for her willingness to go to bat for me.

Mentor as facilitator

I have heard that it takes three years minimum to learn a job: one year to learn the job, another year to do the job, and a third year to fix everything you destroyed during your first two years. In essence, you don't pay dividends until your fourth year on the job.

The mentor as a facilitator has the role of speeding up your development on the job so you pay dividends in a shorter period of time. A mentor won't give you everything you need to get the job done, but he or she won't allow you to continuously bump your head in the same position either. A mentor will teach you how to solve problems more independently and confidently, help you master your craft in arenas where others are watching, and point out the areas where your work should be directed so you don't waste time.

Dr. Henry Gore, one of my mentors at Morehouse College, facilitated my problem-solving abilities. Year after year he placed me in environments that helped me build my confidence and self-esteem as it related to mathematics. He called me "Doctor" whenever he referred to me, even though I was just an undergrad, and established an end-goal which I could aspire to. After he was convinced I knew the material, he would then teach me alternative ways to approach problems and issues. By pointing me in the areas where my work should be focused, he cut down on the time frame it took for me to learn my job and taught me how to solve problems more independently.

Mentor as coach

The mentor guides the protégé toward delivering expected performances by encouraging and giving feedback. Serving as a coach, the mentor must be very comfortable with the protégé to the point of challenging his or her efforts or ability.

The last two years have been absolutely difficult for me, as I have experienced the loss of two of my greatest coaches, Mrs. DaLinda Brown Clark and Dean Thomas Blocker. These two individuals believed in me when I didn't realize my own abilities and set my life on a course to forever affect change and growth in others.

Mrs. Brown Clark was a natural mentor and coach, always encouraging and picking out the best in individuals. Her smile warmed your heart and her selfless heart spoke to your consciousness. She never allowed me to expect anything but the best from myself. Both of us were kindred spirits from New Orleans and she immediately noticed my New Orleans dialect when we met. I spent hours in her office practicing the pronunciation of words because she didn't want mispronunciations to be a barrier to my success. Again and again we'd practice phrases and words until I could say them perfectly ("The word is 'that' not 'dat,'" she'd often kindly remind me). I could relay countless other examples of times when she coached me, but there's not enough space to list them all.

My other coach, Thomas Blocker, has been credited with mentoring hundreds of African-American males into medical school. He was an objective scholar who saw through the fog. I could call him any time and he'd make the world all right with me. Even when I entered college and had to enroll in remedial courses, he encouraged me to follow the goals in my heart, even if they didn't include medicine.

I once called Blocker in the middle of the night to express anxiety over my struggles to attain tenure as a professor at Tulane University. He listened patiently and told me that the faculty wasn't properly equipped to evaluate me because of the wide talents I brought to Tulane. He said they could only evaluate me based on their experiences and talents, which were very limited, narrow, and shortsighted. In short, he gave me the gift of confidence by telling me I was an exceptional candidate for tenure, and if they failed to recognize that, it was due to their own ignorance and they didn't deserve me.

What mentoring is not

Mentoring can assume many forms, but one form it can't assume is paternalism. Paternalism is the relationship between unequal parties where one party acts much like a parent does, imposing his or her own will on the other party because he or she knows what's best for the "child."

A true mentor/protégé relationship must be a two-way relationship. In the end, the mentor usually gains and learns as much as the protégé. All of the mentors I had shared a part of themselves with me, and I likewise shared a part of me with them. The mentoring relationship has taught me never to trust the man or woman who only tells me about their success without telling me about their failures. I need to know that you're human, that you've failed, and that you recovered, got up, and achieved.

The relationship between mentor and protégé is a voluntary one, agreed to by both parties involved. Unlike a parent/child relationship, either party can disengage at any time. Whether formal or informal, the mentoring relationship will only work when both parties are engaged, interested, and committed to the process. A relationship built on paternalism will only result in disaster for mentor and protégé alike.

While the primary roles of a mentor encompass certain supportive and guidance traits, there are behaviors and attitudes to avoid in a mentor. As you seek to achieve, you should avoid the persons with the following traits:

• *The person who is never accessible or missing in action.* How can the mentor help or direct you when they're not around? In organizations especially, we often seek to be mentored by those who are most visible. But keep in mind that visible people may be most visible because they're everywhere except spending time with those who considered them mentors.

• *The person who either avoids meeting the protégé's wishes, withholds information, or impedes growth by supervising and managing too closely.* Some people are so competitive they don't know how to properly advise, facilitate, or coach. They're always on a quest to execute and conquer rather than provide service or sharing. My father met with everyone and shared his knowledge liberally, but many mentors hold back their knowledge for fear they will be out-mastered by their pupils. These are the mentors who will eventually see you as a threat and judge you as an enemy. You never want to enter into a relationship with a mentor who is not readily forthcoming with information or guidance. You never want a mentor who is going to compete with you, just as you never want to give them the impression you're competing with them.

- *The person who publicly and constantly criticizes and tears a person down.* I was taught to build up in public and criticize in private. Likewise, a good mentor won't make an example of a protégé in public; all instructions and constructive criticism will occur in private. Trust is the core value of any mentoring relationship. There were people in graduate school I avoided because I didn't need their baseless negative comments about my prospects for achievement. Although they always said they were clowning around with me, I could sense the envy and destructive energy in their statements and actions. Avoid these vipers with all of your ability.

- *The person who lets the protégé get into a situation and then lets him or her sink or swim.* When no one else in the world seems concerned about you, it's the mentor's job to catch you before you hit rock bottom. The protégé should never be left to fend for himself because it's directly counter to what mentoring is: a caring relationship between two people. Don't expect the mentor to hold your hand, but he or she should at least provide you with sustaining information and direction for self-actualization to occur.

The master must be able to mentor in order to teach, and the master must teach. Although some of my father's protégés turned against him in the end, he never took it personally because he knew in his heart that he had attempted to help people. Your help as a mentor cannot be explicitly selfish but your help must emanate from the deep desire to serve. Mentoring is serious business and our children need mentors today like never before.

My father's example of teaching and mentoring has motivated me to do the same. My door is always open to students and my number is listed. I attempt to be accessible to and supportive of all those who see that I can help them.

Everywhere I've gone in my life, there was someone there to help and guide me. Make yourself accessible and goodhearted people will appear to you. People can sense whether your efforts or sincerity are genuine or not.

What comes from the heart speaks to the heart; therefore, we should attempt to find our voices and share them with the world. Your heart will not lie and your audience will take note of your authenticity. Be true to yourself and others will respect you for that. My father is always himself and grants people permission to be themselves. You learn twice by teaching, so find someone to share all the knowledge you have attained over the years.

Becoming a mentor

Mentoring speaks to the adage that says the man who moves mountains does so one pebble at a time.

Mentors are the people who can help all of us reach pinnacles in our lives. Look around and find people you can help and seek those who can help you. Our children at all ages, of all races and genders, need us to be there for them. Big Brothers/Big Sisters of America, Boys & Girls Club, America's Promise, and Teach for America are some of the national organizations that provide a framework for systematic mentoring of youth. Search locally, at a school or playground. Volunteers are needed to mentor youth and provide them with a stable and constructive relationship. Professionally, there are always opportunities to mentor if you're interested in helping someone other than yourself progress. By helping others, you help yourself: As they succeed and achieve, they'll always acknowledge you and take a part of you along for the ride. We can't all be kings and queens, but we can all attempt to play a role in developing the kings and queens of tomorrow.

But if we're going to change the world, our communities, or our organizations, we must first commit to growing and changing ourselves for the better. Personal introspection and growth is probably the ultimate challenge facing mankind. Looking within and dealing with our own personal shortcomings is where our journey must begin. We live in a society where Blame is the Game and all of our problems are of someone else's making. I refuse to give someone that much power and control over my existence, so I ask myself daily what I can do to make my existence better on this earth regardless of the societal and economic constraints that exist. I see the proverbial "elephant in the room" and I'm committed to going over, around, or through it to achieve my dreams and happiness.

- -

"We must become the change we want to see in the world."

— Mahatma Gandhi

- -

We can change the world by changing ourselves and then reaching back for that one pebble, reaching out to another individual personally and professionally. Commit to being a shining example for the world.

I will never forget what my mother said when I told her I wanted to be a teacher: "If you're going to be a teacher, teach the world a better way. The world is your classroom." The world is all of our classrooms; let's teach it a better way by first mastering ourselves. As we overcome our fears, liberate our potential, become masters, and teach others, unknowingly we become the shining examples that others see that empower and inspire them.

By climbing onto a roof and living his dreams in spite of his shortcomings and societal barriers, Willie Mackie Sr. has liberated others and touched lives yet unborn. I hope his "View from the Roof" has done the same for you.

"Our deepest fear is not that we are inadequate. Our deepest fear is that we are powerful beyond measure. It is our light, not our darkness, that most frightens us. We ask ourselves: who am I to be brilliant, gorgeous, talented and fabulous? Actually, who are you NOT to be? You are a child of God. Your playing small doesn't serve the world. There's nothing enlightened about shrinking so that other people won't feel insecure around you. We were born to make manifest the glory of God that is within us. It's not just in some of us; it's in everyone and as we let our own light shine, we unconsciously give other people permission to do the same. As we are liberated from our own fear, our presence automatically liberates others."*

– Nelson Mandela

---

* This quote isn't from Nelson Mandela, but he often recites it, and credit is often given to him. The quote actually comes from Marianne Williamson's *A Return to Love: Reflections on the Principles of a Course in Miracles.* New York: Harper Collins, 1992. p. 190.

About the Author

Dr. Calvin Mackie is a member of Phi Beta Kappa, a tenured Associate Professor of mechanical engineering at Tulane University, and President of Channel Zer0, an educational and motivational consulting firm founded initially to address the problem of poor academic performance among many of the nation's students (www.channelzro. com).

In his 15 years on the platform, Dr. Mackie has become one of the nation's most prolific and electrifying motivational speakers, delivering more than 500 presentations to high school and college students on the importance of making science, mathematics, and engineering a central part of their education. He is a national spokesman for achievement in the fields of science, business, and technology, and has worked with organizations such as DuPont, Ernst & Young LLP, and NASA to help make their work environments more diverse and conducive to achievement.

In May 2004, Dr. Mackie received a Presidential Award for his leadership in providing greater opportunities for women, minorities, and disabled persons in the fields of science, mathematics, and engineering. He is an active member of the National Speakers Association and many civic and youth centered organizations. He has a B.S. in mathematics from Morehouse College, and B.S, M.S. & Ph.D. in mechanical engineering from Georgia Tech.

Dr. Mackie currently resides in New Orleans with his wife and two sons. *A View from the Roof* is his first book.

Invite Dr. Mackie to speak at your organization, community group, or sales force! For more information on his programs, please visit www.calvinmackie.com.

If you loved *A View from the Roof,* you'll be inspired by these other motivational titles by Dr. Calvin Mackie.

Save the Cheetah Cubs (CD)

In this speech (44 min.), Dr. Mackie presents a metaphor from wildlife that provides insight into one of our most pressing problems, "how can we protect and guide our young people." By exploring the threats, enemies, and survival strategies of baby cheetahs, Dr. Mackie unlocks solutions for how each and every one of us can save our own "Cheetah Cubs."

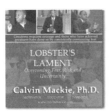

Lobster's Lament (CD)

In this speech (47 min.), Dr. Mackie further explores the lessons of the natural world by defining a critical dilemma faced by developing lobsters. The developing lobster can either choose to face uncertainty in order to grow and lead a full life, or remain in a "comfort zone" and perish. Like the developing lobster, we also have a choice. What will it be?

Free Willie (DVD or CD)

Free Willie is one of Dr. Mackie's most popular speeches. He has been delivering this thoughtful and insightful motivational talk since 1997. In the speech Dr. Mackie challenges the young and old alike to define what it means to be free. He challenges you to truly tap your creative potential and move beyond the social barriers. You have got to get this program!

Achieving Personal Greatness (DVD)

In this speech (42 min.), Dr. Mackie inspires the young and old to tap into their unique purpose and lead more fulfilling and meaningful lives. The event, hosted by the Dupont Corporation, celebrates the vision, leadership, and dedication of Dr. Martin Luther King Jr.

GET THESE AND CALVIN'S OTHER PRODUCTS AT
www.calvinmackie.com
OR ORDER BY PHONE
(504) 391-0730

Dow
gift